101 Python Challenges

- With Solutions / Code Listings -

Philippe Kerampran

101Computing.net

About the Author

Philippe Kerampran has worked as an ICT & Computer Science teacher in a comprehensive UK High School/Academy & 6th Form Centre since 2006. As a Head of Department he has introduced a computing curriculum and computer science courses at GCSE and A Level. He is passionate about finding ways to share his enjoyment of computing with students while developing their abilities to become independent and resourceful learners.

First Printing: 2017

ISBN: 978-1-326-94834-4

Published by:

101 Computing
Email: info@101Computing.net
Website: www.101Computing.net

101 Computing
.net

Picture Credits:
Public Domain pictures from Wikimedia Commons - http://commons.wikimedia.org

Ordering Information:
Special discounts are available on quantity purchases by corporations, associations, educators, and others. For details, contact the publisher at info@101Computing.net.

"I think everybody in this country should learn how to program a computer because it teaches you how to think."

_____

Steve Jobs
Apple Co-founder

Contents at a Glance

101 Programming Challenges

Introduction

By chosing this book, you have embarked on an exciting journey to learn or to improve your coding skills using the Python programming language. So welcome on board!

Coding knowledge is nowadays considered as a must-have 21st century skill. The world we live in is surrounded by computer algorithms. These can be found not only in computing devices and smartphones but also in everyday objects through the use of embedded technologies. This includes cars, house appliances, wearable technologies as well as robotics and drones. All of these technologies are controlled by computer algorithms. So effectively we can say that coding is the new buzz language of today's tech-savvy world.

One of the main reasons for developing your coding knowledge is that, as Steve Jobs described it, learning how to code "teaches you how to think". Effectively, while designing and writing your own computer algorithms, you are going to develop your analytical skills, creative thinking skills, problem solving and troubleshooting skills. You will also apply other essential maths and science based knowledge to your algorithms.

The purpose of this book is to bring together a collection of 101 challenges that will help you develop your Python coding skills as well as your computational knowledge. This selection of challenges from the 101computing.net blog will cover the essential skills used in procedural programming, focusing on the key programming constructs: sequencing, selection and iteration. You will find out more about these programming concepts in the first three chapters of this book and you will apply these in all of the 101 challenges.

How to use this book?

This book is targeted at both learners and educators who want to find a challenging and enthusing approach to develop their programming skills using Python.

As a learner...

The 101 challenges are organised into ten chapters. If you are fairly new to coding, I would recommend you to complete these chapters in order as each chapter will introduce new programming concepts that you will need to be confident with before moving on to the next chapter. If you are fairly confident with your programming skills, you can complete these challenges in any order following your own interests.

Each challenge is solved and the book gives you the full code listing. As you progress through the book, I do recommend you to have a go at trying to solve the challenges first before looking at the given code. You may want to use the code when you are stuck and not sure how to progress further. Once you have completed a challenge, you can also compare your code with the given solution.

Looking at existing code is good practice. It enables you to pick up new programming concepts and approaches. Reverse engineering a piece of code helps you get a good understanding of how the code works and of how it can be used to solve different problems. So, do spend time analysing the given code to make sure you fully understand it. See if you can adapt the given solutions or try your own approaches by writing your own algorithms too as you may find more effective ways to solve these challenges.

Python is a fantastic free and open-source programming language. You will need a few hours to complete the first few challenges to get used to the syntax of this language. Before your start, always remember that Python is a case sensitive language and that it complies with the off-side rule: in other words Python is "space-sensitive" and uses indentation especially when using selection, iteration and sub-routines. By completing all these challenges you will enjoy discovering the functionalities and characteristics of this programming language. It is the perfect language to start learning how to code. But don't be fooled: this language is not just

10

used for education purposes. It is also widely used in the industry to create desktop applications, mobile apps and server side scripts for web-based applications. Though this book focuses on procedural programming, Python is also an Object Oriented language. I decided to briefly introduce this concept in the last challenge; however Object Oriented programming is beyond the scope of this book. As an introduction to programming, it is essential to be very confident with procedural programming before moving on to Object Oriented programming which would be necessary to build more complex systems.

As an educator/teacher...

For educators this book can be used in many different ways. You may be running a computing club and want to find exciting challenges for students to complete together or compete against each other. Alternatively you can decide to focus on one of these challenges with your class and approach it with a more directed step by step approach to help pupils discover new skills. Or you can use some of these challenges as homework tasks. Note that all of the 101 challenges, as well as many other challenges, are available on the 101computing.net blog, though most of the times without the full solution / code listing.

You will probably find out that when teaching larger groups, the ability of students to grasp computing concepts varies widely. This is why I believe you should allow for some differentiation by selecting different challenges for different learners based on their abilities. The main philosophy behind the 101computing.net blog and behind this book is to **challenge rather than instruct.** For learners to become good computer scientists they need to be able to acquire new skills by themselves. On occasions you may want to give students the full code listing for them to work on, analyse and reverse-engineer. On other occasions you will prefer not to give them the full solution. You may instead produce some step by step instructions (just enough to get them started) or encourage them to research the web. There are billions of resources on the web and learners need to be able to use these effectively to acquire new skills and become independent learners. When learners are really stuck, encourage them to work collaboratively, to review and discuss each other's code. If they are still stuck, advise them to look at their previous projects or point them in the right direction towards an online resource that may help them get unstuck. Focus on the process more than the actual outcome. If your learners become **more independent and resourceful learners** then praise yourself for being a fantastic teacher!

Recommended Resources:

You are nearly ready to get started with your first challenge. And the good news is that, provided you have internet access, you will not need to install anything on your computer to get started. Except from challenge 101, all of the other challenges can be completed online using the web address given for each challenge (also accessible using the QR codes provided). Each web address points towards the blog post of the challenge and each bog post includes a widget from trinket.io, an online Python environment that lets you type and run Python code within your web browser.

If you are serious about coding, you will most likely want to install Python on your own computer. We would also strongly recommend that you investigate installing a Python IDE (integrated Development Environment). There are several free Python IDEs available, but if you are not sure which one to choose from, we shall recommend PyScripter which is a free, open-source IDE. It will make it a lot easier to type your code (Syntax highlighting and checking as you type, indentation options...) and to troubleshoot and debug your code using the built-in debugging tools (breakpoints, variables windows...).

You will not be able to complete the last challenge (101) online as it requires you to access the Pygame library, not available on trinket.io. So, for this last challenge, you will need to install Python as well as the Pygame library using the links provided below.

Python *Version 3.6.0 or above*	https://www.python.org/downloads/
PyScripter IDE	https://en.wikipedia.org/wiki/PyScripter
Pygame – Python Library	http://www.pygame.org

Beyond the Book:

The 101 challenges from this book are just a selection from a wider range of programming and computing challenges from the 101computing.net blog. I am regularly posting and amending existing challenges on this blog so do not hesitate to visit the blog on a regular basis.

You can also register on the blog or follow me on different social networks to be kept informed when new blog posts are being published:

101Computing.net Blog	http://www.101computing.net/
Twitter	https://twitter.com/101computing
Facebook	https://www.facebook.com/101Computing/
Youtube	https://www.youtube.com/c/101Computing

I would like to hear from you:

You may be willing to give me feedback on this book or on my blog or have suggestions on how I could improve these resources further. I would love to hear what you have to say. Do not hesitate to contact me through the social networks listed above or via e-mail: info@101computing.net.

And now?

Well that's it, let's get coding. You are ready to move on to challenge #1.

Happy coding!

Chapter #1: Getting Started

Let's get started with our first few challenges. Though these challenges will be based on fairly basic algorithms (based on sequencing), these will enable you to get used to the Python syntax as well as cover a range of key programming concepts that are essential and heavily used in most, if not all programs.

When working on these first challenges, bear in mind that the computer will run your code one line at a time from the top (line 1) to the end of your program. This is what we call **sequencing**.

Our first few challenges will cover the following programming techniques:

- Sequencing,
- Input / Output,
- Variables,
- Data Types,
- Casting Variables,
- Assignment Operator,
- Arithmetic Operators.

1. My Superhero

In this challenge we are learning how to use variables to store the properties of a superhero. At this stage all our variables will be used to store a piece of text (string) such as the name of our superhero or their super power.

Once we have stored all the properties of our superhero we will use the print command in Python to print a full description of our superhero.

Web Address
http://www.101computing.net/my-superhero/

Python Code

```
1.  # My superhero - www.101computing.net/my-superhero/
2.
3.  #Store the properties of your superhero
4.  name = "Baymax"
5.  nickname = "Balloon Man"
6.  superPower = "provide assistance to injured people"
7.  weapon = "rocket fist"
8.  occupation = "nurse"
9.  allies = "Hiro, Honey, Wasabi, Fred, Go Go Tomago"
10. enemy = "Yokai"
11. weakness = "deflatable"
12. location = "San Fransokyo"
13.
14. #Display a description of your superhero
15. print("#############################")
16. print("#                           #")
17. print("#       MY SUPERHERO        #")
18. print("#                           #")
19. print("#############################")
20. print("")
21. print("I am  "+ name + ", and my nickname is " + nickname +
    ".")
22. print("My super power is that I can " + superPower + ".")

23. print("However my weakness is that I am " + weakness + ".")

24. print("My allies are " + allies + " and my enemy is " + enem
    y + ".")
25. print("I live in " + location + ".")
```

2. Cake Sale

We are organising a cake sale and want to predict how much money we will raise. During this cake sale, we will be selling three types of cakes:

1. cupcakes at 40p each,
2. macarons at 50p each,
3. cheesecakes at 70p each.

Our Python program will estimate how much money can be raised when selling these cakes based on the quantity of cakes we expect to sell.

Web Address

http://www.101computing.net/cake-sale/

Python Code

```
1.  #Cake Sale Challenge - www.101computing.net/cake-sale
2.  cupcakePrice = 0.40
3.  macaronPrice = 0.50
4.  cheesecakePrice = 0.70
5.
6.  #Step 1: Input
7.  cupcakes = int(input("How many cupcakes do you plan to sell?
    "))
8.  macarons = int(input("How many macarons do you plan to sell?
    "))
9.  cheesecakes = int(input("How many cheese cakes do you plan t
    o sell?"))
10.
11. #Step 2: Process
12. total = (cupcakePrice * cupcakes) + (macaronPrice * macarons
    ) + (cheesecakePrice * cheesecakes)
13.
14. #Step 3: Output - Display result with two decimal places
15. print("You will raise £" + str("%.2f" % total))
```

3. Lightning Distance Calculator

Have you ever seen a lightning flash or heard the
thunder of lightning and wondered how close you
were from the lightning strike? Have you noticed that
there often was a delay between the flash of light and the clap of thunder
when a lightning occurs?

It is possible to calculate the distance to a lightning strike by counting the
seconds between the lightning flash and the sound of thunder.

When lightning strikes, the first thing you see is the flash of light which
you can see instantly. This is because light travels at a very high speed
(Speed of light = 300,000 km/s). At the same time a clap of thunder is
created. However, in the air a sound wave does not travel as fast as light,
so it may take a few seconds for this clap of thunder to reach you. This
depends on how far you are from the lightning.

Look at the following diagram and check the formula of speed. Bear in
mind that the speed of a sound wave in the air is 340 m/s.

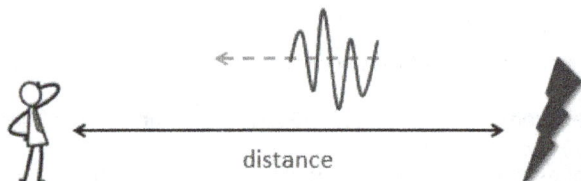

distance

$$speed = \frac{distance}{time}$$

$$distance = speed \times time$$

For this challenge we will write a Python program that asks the end-user to enter a number of seconds. The program should then calculate and output the distance (in kilometres) from the lightning strike. As 1 mile = 1.609 km, we will also convert and display this distance in miles.

Web Address

http://www.101computing.net/lightning-distance-calculator/

Python Code

```
1.  #Ligthning Distance Calculator -
    www.101computing.net/lightning-distance-calculator/
2.
3.  speedOfSound = 340 #m/s
4.
5.  #Input
6.  time = int(input("How many seconds did you count between the
    lightning flash and the clap of thunder?"))
7.
8.  #Process
9.  distance = time * speedOfSound
10.
11. #Output
12. print("The ligthning strike occured " + str("%.1f" % (distan
    ce/1000)) + "km away.")
13. print("The ligthning strike occured " + str("%.1f" % (distan
    ce/1609)) + " miles away.")
```

4. Discount Price Calculator

Shopping during the sales can sometimes be very confusing. With discounted prices at 10%, 20%, 50% or even 70%!

For this challenge we are going to write a Python program that prompts the user to enter a price in pounds (or in your own currency) (e.g. £90) and a discount rate to apply (e.g. 20%).

Our program will then calculate and display the discounted price.

Python Code

```
1.  # Discount Price Calculator - www.101computing.net/discount-
    price-calculator/
2.
3.  #Step1: Retrieving user inputs
4.  itemPrice = float(input("What is the price of the item?"))
5.  percentageDiscount = float(input("What is the percentage dis
    count?"))
6.
7.  #Step2: Processing
8.  reducedPrice = itemPrice-itemPrice*percentageDiscount/100
9.
10. #Step 3: Displaying the price to two decimal places
11. print("The reduced price is £" + str("%.2f" % reducedPrice))
```

Chapter #2: What if...

In the previous challenges we used sequencing, which is based on the idea that a computer program starts at line 1, reads and executes the line and progresses to the next line, and so on until it reaches the last line of the program.

We are now going to investigate **selection** using IF statements. Selection allows the computer to choose alternative pathways by bypassing a few lines of code if a condition is not met.

In the next challenges we will use:

- Selection using IF Statements,
- Nested IF Statements,
- Comparison Operators,
- Boolean Operators.

IF ELIF ELSE

<= < > >= != ==

AND OR NOT

5. House For Sale

Building up from the previous challenges you will now use variables to store information to describe your house. You will use different data types for your variables. Some of your variables will be used to store text (string) such as the location/address of your house. Some variables will be used to store numbers, either whole numbers (integers) or numbers with a decimal place (reals/floats). For instance we could use a variable called numberOfBedrooms (integer) and a variable to store the price (Real number). Finally you will also store True or False values (Boolean) for instance to describe whether or not your house has a garage.

Once you have stored all the characteristics of your house you will use the print command in Python to print a full description of your house.

Web Address
http://www.101computing.net/for-sale/

Python Code

```
1.  # House for sale - www.101computing.net/for-sale/
2.
3.  # Store the characteristics of your house using variables
4.  #Variables used to store text (String)
5.  typeOfHouse = "detached"
6.  location = "Brighton"
7.  equipment = "central heating"
8.
9.  #Variables used to store whole numbers (integer)
10. numberOfBedrooms = 3
11. numberOfFloors = 2
12.
13. #Variables used to store true/false values (Boolean)
14. hasGarage = True
15. hasConservatory = False
16.
17. #Variables used to store decimal numbers (real/float)
18. price = 149999.90
19.
20. #Display a description of your house
21. print("############################")
```

```
22. print("#                              #")
23. print("#            FOR SALE          #")
24. print("#                              #")
25. print("##############################")
26. print("")
27. print("A lovely " + typeOfHouse + " house located in " + loc
    ation + ".")
28. print("This house has " + str(numberOfBedrooms) + " bedrooms
    .")
29. if (numberOfFloors>1):
30.   print("This house consists of " + str(numberOfFloors) + "
    floors.")
31. else:
32.   print("This house is a single-storey house.")
33. if hasGarage==True:
34.   print("This house also has a garage!")
35. if hasConservatory==True:
36.   print("This house also has a conservatory!")
37. print("This house is also equipped with " + equipment + ".")

38. #Display price, using 2 decimal places
39. print("This house is on sale for £" +str("%.2f" % price))
```

6.   Hogwarts Sorting Hat Challenge

In the Harry Potter series of novels written by British author J. K. Rowling, The Sorting Hat is a magical hat at Hogwarts that determines which of the four school Houses each new student belongs most to. These four Houses are Gryffindor, Hufflepuff, Ravenclaw, and Slytherin.

In this challenge we are going to write Python program to control the Sorting Hat. Our algorithm will be based on the following flowchart:

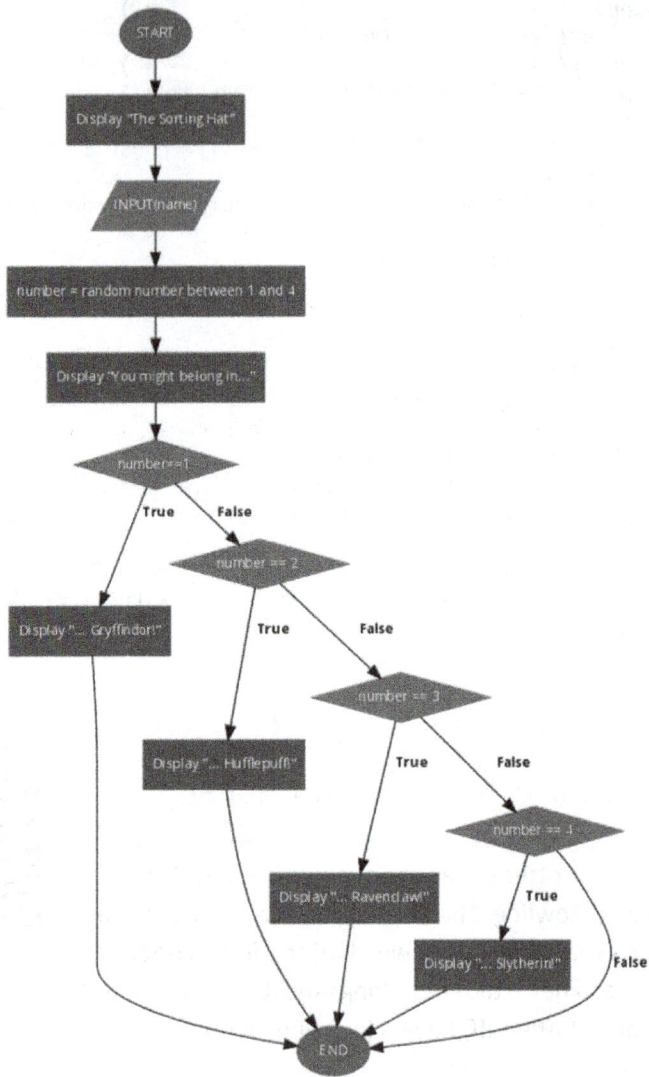

START

Display "The Sorting Hat"

INPUT(name)

number = random number between 1 and 4

Display "You might belong in..."

number==1
- True → Display "... Gryffindor!"
- False → number == 2
  - True → Display "... Hufflepuff"
  - False → number == 3
    - True → Display "... Ravenclaw"
    - False → number == 4
      - True → Display "... Slytherin!"
      - False

END

Web Address	
http://www.101computing.net/hogwarts-sorting-hat-challenge/	

Python Code	
1.	#The Sorting Hat - www.101computing.net/hogwarts-sorting-hat-challenge/
2.	import random

```
3.
4.   print("--- The Sorting Hat ---")
5.   #Input
6.   name = input("What's your name?")
7.
8.   #Generate random number
9.   number = random.randint(1,4)
10.
11.  #Output
12.  print("You might belong in...")
13.  if number==1:
14.     print("... Gryffindor!")
15.  elif number == 2:
16.     print("... Hufflepuff!")
17.  elif number == 3:
18.     print("... Ravenclaw!")
19.  elif number == 4:
20.     print("... Slytherin!")
```

7. Meet E.V.E.

Computer algorithms are essential for robots to
function as expected and interact with human beings.
For this challenge, we will write a computer program to
enable a robot to chat with a human being. This is a form of Artificial
Intelligence! Our robot will be called E.V.E. and will ask the user a few
questions. It will then analyse possible user answers to respond to the
user with predefined possible answers.

Web Address

http://www.101computing.net/meet-eve/

Python Code

```
1.   #Meet Eve - www.101computing.net/meet-eve
2.
3.   #Introduction
4.   print("Hello my name is E.V.E. I am a computer algorithm.")

5.   name = input("What is your name?")
6.   print("Hello " + name + ".")
```

```
7.  print("Nice to meet you")
8.
9.  #Would you like to talk to me?
10. talk = input("Would you like to chat with me?").lower()
11. if talk=="yes":
12.    print("Cool, I love chatting with human beings.")
13. elif talk=="no":
14.    print("Ok, it was nice to meet you. Bye for now.")
15.    #Stop the program:
16.    exit()
17. else:
18.    print("Not sure I know what you meant but will talk to you
       anyway.")
19.
20. #print an empty line
21. print("")
22.
23. #Music
24. band = input("What's your favourite band?").lower()
25. if band=="1d" or band=="1 direction" or band=="one direction
    ":
26.    print("Oh no... not One direction!")
27. elif band=="coldplay":
28.    print("Yes, that's my favourite band too.")
29. elif band=="snow patrol" or band=="oasis" or band=="the beat
    les":
30.    print("I like this band too, but I prefer Coldplay")
31. else:
32.    print("Ok. I don't know this band. Mine is Coldplay.")
33.
34. #print an empty line
35. print("")
36.
37. #Car Brand
38. car = input("What's your favourite car brand?").lower()
39. if car=="audi" or car=="bmw" or car=="mercedes":
40.    print("I like German cars too! They have a very nice desig
       n!")
41. elif car=="ferrari" or car=="porsche" or car=="lamborghini":
42.    print("Sports car are my favourite cars too!")
43. elif car=="tesla":
44.    print("Electric cars are great for the environment!")
45. else:
46.    print("Ok. My favourite car is the Google car.")
47.
48. #print an empty line
49. print("")
50.
```

```
51. print("Thanks " + name + ". It was very nice to talk to you.
    ")
52. print("Bye for now.")
```

8. Voting Age Checker

For this challenge we are going to code a script to ask a user how old they are and inform them as to whether they are old enough to vote or not. If they are not old enough to vote, the script will calculate how many years the user will have to wait before being allowed to vote.

Web Address
http://www.101computing.net/voting-age-checker-flowchart/

Python Code

```
1.  #Voting Age Checker - http://www.101computing.net/voting-
    age-checker-flowchart/
2.
3.  print(" --- Voting Age Checker! --- ")
4.  age=int(input("What is your age?"))
5.
6.  if age >= 18:
7.     print("You can vote.")
8.  else:
9.     gap=18-age
10.    print("You will be able to vote in " + str(gap) + " years"
       )
```

9. What's My Grade?

This challenge consists of creating a user friendly program that asks a user to input their exam score out of 60 marks. The program should output the grade that they have received using the grade boundaries listed in the table below:

Mark	Grade
54+	A*
48 – 53	A
42 – 47	B
36 – 41	C
30 – 35	D
24 – 29	E
0 – 23	U

Web Address

http://www.101computing.net/whats-my-grade/

Python Code

```
1.  #What's my grade? - http://www.101computing.net/whats-my-
    grade/
2.
3.  print("#############################################")
4.  print("#                                           #")
5.  print("#          Exam Grade Calculator            #")
6.  print("#                                           #")
7.  print("#############################################")
8.  print("")
9.
10. marks = int(input("How many marks did you get (0-60)?"))
11.
12. if marks>60 or marks<0:
13.   print("Sorry, this is not a valid score!")
14. elif (marks>=54 and marks<=60):
15.   print("Wow you have an A* grade!")
16. elif (marks>=48) and (marks<=53):
17.   print("Great you have an A grade!")
18. elif (marks>=42) and (marks<=47):
19.   print("You did well, you have a B grade!")
20. elif (marks>=36) and (marks<=41):
21.   print("You have secured a C grade!")
22. elif (marks>=30) and (marks<=35):
23.   print("You have reached a D grade!")
24. elif (marks>=24) and (marks<=29):
25.   print("You have an E grade!")
26. else:
27.   print("Unlucky you have a U grade!")
```

10. How Eco-Friendly Are You?

It would not be hot news for you to hear that throughout your everyday life, whatever you do, you are having an impact on the environment. Words like pollution, global warming, carbon dioxide, recycling, energy saving, waste reduction are no mystery to you.

For this challenge you are going to design a quiz that people can take to find out how green or eco-friendly they are. The quiz will consist of eight questions and will be used to give the end-user a score.

All eight questions and possible answers are listed at the web address provided below.

At the end of the quiz, the user will be told what their score is and what category they belong to amongst these four categories:

- Negative score (<0) - Amber Category,
- Between 0 and 100 - Light Green Category,
- Between 101 and 200 - Emerald Green Category,
- Above 200 - Deep Green Category.

Web Address
http://www.101computing.net/how-eco-friendly-are-you/

Python Code
```
1.  # Take the eco-friendly quiz - www.101computing.net/how-eco-
    friendly-are-you/
2.  print("~~~~~~~~~~~~~~~~~~~~~~~~~~~~~~~~~~~~~")
3.  print("~   The eco-friendly quiz    ~")
4.  print("~~~~~~~~~~~~~~~~~~~~~~~~~~~~~~~~~~~~~")
5.  print("\nInstructions: Answer each question of this test acc
    urately. Be honest with your answers.")
6.  print("At the end you will be given your eco-
    score that tells you how eco-friendly you are!")
7.  print("You will be able to compare this score with your frie
    nds and hopefully be inspired to change your daily routines
    and become even more eco-friendly!")
```

```
8.
9. ecoScore = 0
10.
11. print("\nQuestion 1:")
12. print("How do you come to school every day?")
13. answer = input("1 - By car, 2 - By bus or train, 3 -
    On foot, 4 - On your bike or scooter?")
14. if answer=="1":
15.     ecoScore -= 50
16. elif answer=="2":
17.     ecoScore -= 10
18. elif answer=="3" or answer=="4":
19.     ecoScore += 100
20. else:
21.     print("Not a valid answer.")
22.
23. print("\nQuestion 2:")
24. print("How often did you take the plane over the last 12 mon
    ths?")
25. answer = input("1 - None, 2 - Once, 3 - Twice, 4 -
    At least three times")
26. if answer=="1":
27.     ecoScore += 100
28. elif answer=="2":
29.     ecoScore -= 25
30. elif answer=="3":
31.     ecoScore -= 50
32. elif answer=="4":
33.     ecoScore -= 100
34. else:
35.     print("Not a valid answer.")
36.
37. print("\nQuestion 3:")
38. print("Do you use your recycling bins at home?")
39. answer = input("1 - Never, 2 - Rarely, 3 - Often, 4 -
    Every day")
40. if answer=="1":
41.     ecoScore -= 50
42. elif answer=="2":
43.     ecoScore += 10
44. elif answer=="3":
45.     ecoScore += 50
46. elif answer=="4":
47.     ecoScore += 100
48. else:
49.     print("Not a valid answer.")
50.
51. print("\nQuestion 4:")
52. print("When you go shopping do you...")
```

```
53. answer = input("1 -
    Bring your own reusable carrier bags, 2 -
    Ask for plastic bags")
54. if answer=="1":
55.     ecoScore += 20
56. elif answer=="2":
57.     ecoScore -= 20
58. else:
59.     print("Not a valid answer.")
60.
61. print("\nQuestion 5:")
62. print("Do you use energy saving bulbs?")
63. answer = input("1 - Yes, 2 - No")
64. if answer=="1":
65.     ecoScore += 30
66. elif answer=="2":
67.     ecoScore -= 30
68. else:
69.     print("Not a valid answer.")
70.
71. print("\nQuestion 6:")
72. print("When you clean your teeth, do you let the water run?"
    )
73. answer = input("1 - Yes, 2 - Sometimes, 3 - No, never")
74. if answer=="1":
75.     ecoScore -= 30
76. elif answer=="2":
77.     ecoScore -= 10
78. elif answer=="3":
79.     ecoScore += 20
80. else:
81.     print("Not a valid answer.")
82.
83. print("\nQuestion 7:")
84. print("is your house fitted with solar panels?")
85. answer = input("1 - yes, 2 - no,")
86. if answer=="1":
87.     ecoScore += 100
88. elif answer=="2":
89.     ecoScore += 0
90. else:
91.     print("Not a valid answer.")
92.
93. print("\nQuestion 8:")
94. print("when it gets cold do you..?")
95. answer = input("1 - Put on a blanket or jumper, 2 -
    Turn the heater on")
96. if answer=="1":
97.     ecoScore += 50
```

```
98. elif answer=="2":
99.     ecoScore -= 50
100.else:
101.    print("Not a valid answer.")
102.
103.#Display feedback based on total score
104.print("\nEnd of Quiz\n")
105.print("Your eco-score is: " + str(ecoScore) + " points.")
106.if (ecoScore<0):
107.    print("You are amber!")
108.elif (ecoScore>=0) and (ecoScore<=100):
109.    print("You are light green!")
110.elif (ecoScore>=101) and (ecoScore<=200):
111.    print("You are emerald green!")
112.elif (ecoScore>200):
113.    print("You are deep green!")
```

11. Fahrenheit to Celsius Converter

Degree Fahrenheit (°F) and Degree Celsius (°C) are the main two units to measure temperature. The Fahrenheit scale is used mainly in the USA whereas other countries tend to use the Celsius scale. It is possible to convert a temperature from Celsius degrees to Fahrenheit and vice-versa using the following conversion formulas:

$$°C = (°F - 32) \times 5 / 9$$

$$°F = (°C \times 9 / 5) + 32$$

For this challenge we will write a Python program to:

1. Ask the end-user whether they want to convert from Fahrenheit to Celsius or from Celsius to Fahrenheit,
2. Ask the user to enter a temperature in the correct unit,

3. Apply the conversion formula and display the temperature in the new unit.

Web Address
http://www.101computing.net/fahrenheit-to-celsius-converter/

Python Code

```
1.  #Fahrenheit to Celsius converter -
    www.101computing.net/fahrenheit-to-celsius-converter/
2.
3.  print("Would you like to convert:")
4.  print(" 1 - From Fahrenheit to Celsius?")
5.  print(" 2 - From Celsius to Fahrenheit?")
6.  option = input("Type 1 or 2:")
7.
8.  if option=="1":
9.    #From Fahrenheit to Celsius
10.   fahrenheit = float(input("Enter  temperature in Degree Fah
    renheit:"))
11.   celsius = (fahrenheit - 32) * 5 / 9
12.   celsius = round(celsius,1)
13.   print(str(fahrenheit) + " Degrees Fahrenheit = " + str(cel
    sius) + " Degrees Celsius")
14. elif option=="2":
15.   #From Celsius to Fahrenheit
16.   celsius = float(input("Enter  temperature in Degree Celsiu
    s:"))
17.   fahrenheit = (celsius * 9 / 5) + 32
18.   fahrenheit = round(fahrenheit,1)
19.   print(str(celsius) + " Degrees Celsius = " + str(fahrenhei
    t) + " Degrees Fahrenheit")
20. else:
21.   print("Invalid option!")
```

12. My Library

For this challenge you will work for the librarian who needs a computer program to help pupils find out where books can be found in the library.

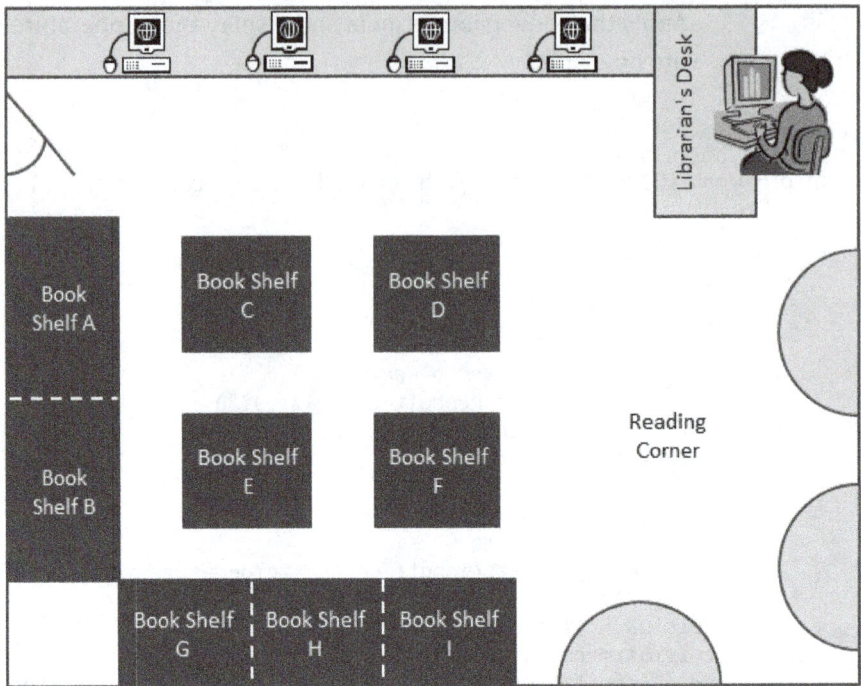

The library contains nine bookshelves labelled from A to I. Each bookshelf specialises in one genre. For instance, bookshelf A is for comedy fiction books. The Science and Technology section of the library is also organised in five sub-sections as follows:

- H1: Biology Books
- H2: Physics Books
- H3: Chemistry Books
- H4: Computer Science Books
- H5: Design & Technology Books

Below is the list of bookshelves and genres:

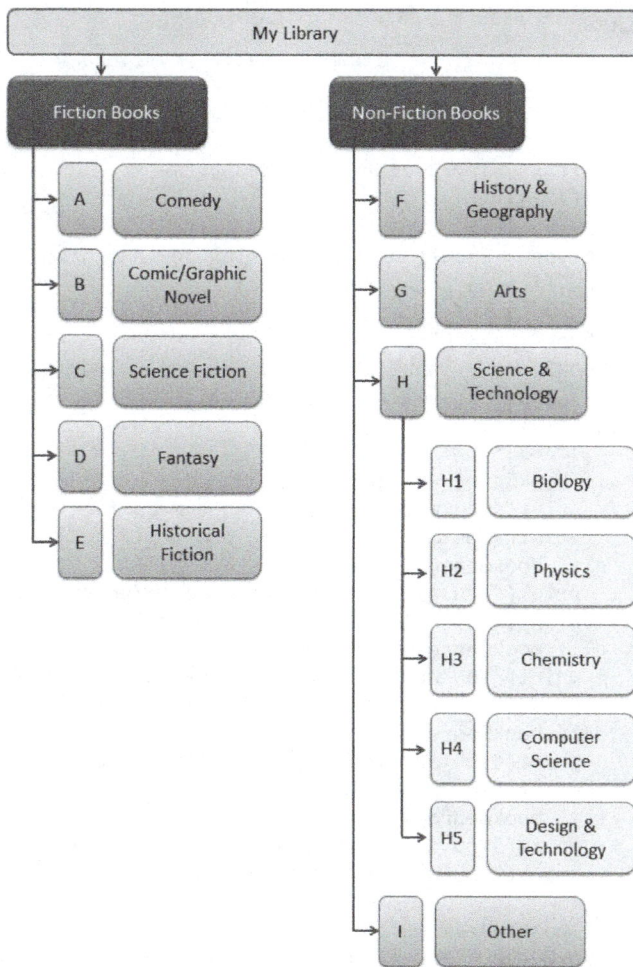

My Library

Fiction Books
- A — Comedy
- B — Comic/Graphic Novel
- C — Science Fiction
- D — Fantasy
- E — Historical Fiction

Non-Fiction Books
- F — History & Geography
- G — Arts
- H — Science & Technology
  - H1 — Biology
  - H2 — Physics
  - H3 — Chemistry
  - H4 — Computer Science
  - H5 — Design & Technology
- I — Other

Our task is to write a computer program that asks the user if they are looking for a fiction or a non-fiction book. Based on the user answer the program will ask the user to choose the genre from a list of available genres. Finally the program will return the location (A to I) of books of this genre.

Web Address

http://www.101computing.net/my-library/

```
1.  #My Library - www.101computing.net/my-library
2.
3.  print("##########################")
4.  print("#        My Library        #")
5.  print("##########################")
6.  print("")
7.
8.  bookType = input("Are you looking for a fiction (type F) or
    a non-fiction book (type NF)?")
9.
10. if bookType=="F":
11.   bookGenre = input("What genre are you looking for: comedy
      (1), graphic novel (2), science fiction (3), fantasy (4), hi
      storial fiction (5)?")
12.
13.   if bookGenre == "1":
14.     print("You are looking for a comedy fiction book.")
15.     print("You will find it in bookshelf A.")
16.   elif bookGenre == "2":
17.     print("You are looking for a comic/graphic novel.")
18.     print("You will find it in bookshelf B.")
19.   elif bookGenre == "3":
20.     print("You are looking for a science fiction book.")
21.     print("You will find it in bookshelf c.")
22.   elif bookGenre == "4":
23.     print("You are looking for a fantasy book.")
24.     print("You will find it in bookshelf D.")
25.   elif bookGenre == "5":
26.     print("You are looking for a historial fiction book.")
27.     print("You will find it in bookshelf E.")
28.
29. elif bookType=="NF":
30.   bookGenre = input("What genre are you looking for: History
      and Geography (1), Arts (2), Science and Technology (3), Ot
      her (4)")
31.
32.   if bookGenre == "1":
33.     print("You are looking for a History & Geography book.")
34.     print("You will find it in bookshelf F.")
35.   elif bookGenre == "2":
36.     print("You are looking for a Arts Book.")
37.     print("You will find it in bookshelf G.")
38.   elif bookGenre == "3":
39.     print("You are looking for a Science & Technology book."
      )
```

```
40.     sciencebook = input("What type of science book are you l
        ooking for? Biology (1), Physics (2), Chemistry (3), Compute
        r Science (4), Design and Technology (5).")
41.     if sciencebook == "1":
42.         print("You are looking for a Biology Book.")
43.         print("You will find it in bookshelf H1.")
44.     elif sciencebook == "2":
45.         print("You are looking for a Physics Book.")
46.         print("You will find it in bookshelf H2.")
47.     elif sciencebook == "3":
48.         print("You are looking for a Chemistry Book.")
49.         print("You will find it in bookshelf H3.")
50.     elif sciencebook == "4":
51.         print("You are looking for a Computer Science Book.")
52.         print("You will find it in bookshelf H4.")
53.     elif sciencebook == "5":
54.         print("You are looking for a Design and Technology Boo
        k.")
55.         print("You will find it in bookshelf H5.")
56.     elif bookGenre == "4":
57.         print("You are looking for a Other book.")
58.         print("You will find it in bookshelf I.")
```

13. How Old Is Your Cat?

In this challenge we are going to create a cat's age convertor to find out how old a cat is in "human years". To convert the age of a cat in human years we will have to apply the following rules:

- Year 1 counts for 15 Human Years,
- Year 2 counts for 9 Human Years,
- Thereafter each year counts for 4 Human Years.

For example:

- A 1 year old cat is 15 Human Years old,
- A 2 years old cat is 15 + 9 = 24 Human Years old,
- A 3 years old cat is 15 + 9 + 4 = 28 Human Years old,
- A 4 years old cat is 15 + 9 + 4 + 4 = 32 Human Years old,
- A 5 years old cat is 15 + 9 + 4 + 4 + 4= 36 Human Years old.

More specific information is available at the web address provided below to find out the actual age of a kitten (when they are less than one year old) as well as the age boundaries of the different stages of life for cats.

Web Address
http://www.101computing.net/how-old-is-your-cat/

Python Code

```
1.  #Cat's Age Convertor - http://www.101computing.net/how-old-
    is-your-cat/
2.
3.  older = str(input("Is your cat over one year old \n Please a
    nswer Yes or No")).upper()
4.  convertedAge = 0
5.
6.  #Work out the equivalent in human years based on the age of
    the cat:
7.  if older == "YES":
8.    #Your cat i at least 1 year old
9.    years = int(input("How old is your cat (in years)?"))
10.   if years == 1:
11.     convertedAge = 15
12.   elif years == 2:
13.     convertedAge = 15 + 9
14.   else:
15.     convertedAge = 15 + 9 + ((years - 2) * 4)
16.
17. if older == "NO":
18.   #The cat is less than 1 year old
19.   months = int(input("How old is your cat (in Months)?"))
20.   if months<= 2:
21.     convertedAge = 0.75
22.   elif months == 3:
23.     convertedAge = 2
24.   elif months == 4:
25.     convertedAge = 5
26.   elif months == 5:
27.     convertedAge = 8
28.   elif acm == 6:
29.     convertedAge = 10
30.   elif months < 8:
31.     convertedAge = 13
32.   elif months < 12:
33.     convertedAge = 14
34.   elif months == 12:
35.     convertedAge = 15
```

```
36.
37. #Find out the life stage of ths cat
38. if convertedAge <= 10:
39.     lifeStage = "Kitten"
40. elif  convertedAge > 10 and convertedAge <=24:
41.     lifeStage = "Junior"
42. elif  convertedAge > 24 and convertedAge <= 40:
43.     lifeStage = "Prime"
44. elif  convertedAge > 40 and convertedAge <= 56:
45.     lifeStage = "Mature"
46. elif  convertedAge > 56 and convertedAge <= 72:
47.     lifeStage = "Senior"
48. elif  convertedAge > 72:
49.     lifeStage = "Geriatric"
50.
51. #Display the result (converted age and lifestage) to the end
    -user
52. print("In human years your cat is the equivalent of " + str(
    convertedAge) + " years old. \nYour cat is in the " + lifeSt
    age + " stage of its life.")
```

14. The Window Cleaner's Quote

A window cleaner uses the following pricing policy to
calculate how much to charge for cleaning all the
windows of his customer's dwelling. This pricing policy
is based on the number of windows that need to be cleaned and works as
follows:

- All quoted prices include a fixed call out fee of £10,
- Then, the first five windows are charged at £2 each,
- The next five windows are charged at £1.50 each,
- Any additional windows are charged at £1 each.

Our task is to write a computer program that prompts the end-user to
enter the number of windows of their dwelling. The program will then
calculate the quoted price using the pricing policy described above and
display it to the end-user.

Python Code

```
1.  #The House Cleaner's Quote - www.101computing.net/window-
    cleaner/
2.
3.  numberOfWindows = int(input("How many windows need to be cle
    aned?"))
4.  cost = 10
5.
6.  if numberOfWindows <= 5:
7.      cost = cost + (numberOfWindows * 2)
8.  elif numberOfWindows <= 10:
9.      #First 5 windows at £2 each
10.     cost = cost + (5 * 2)
11.     #Remaining Windows at £1.50 each
12.     windowsLeft = numberOfWindows - 5
13.     cost = cost + (windowsLeft * 1.50)
14. else:
15.     #First 10 windows
16.     cost = cost + (5 * 2) + (5 * 1.50)
17.     #Remaining Windows at £1 each
18.     windowsLeft = numberOfWindows - 10
19.     cost = cost + (windowsLeft * 1)
20.
21. print("Your quoted cost is £" + str(cost))
```

15. Resistors in Series and in Parallel

For this challenge we will create a Python program that will help us calculate the total resistance when two resistors are connected either in series or in parallel.

This program will be based on the following formulas:

Resistors in Series:

Resistors in Parallel:

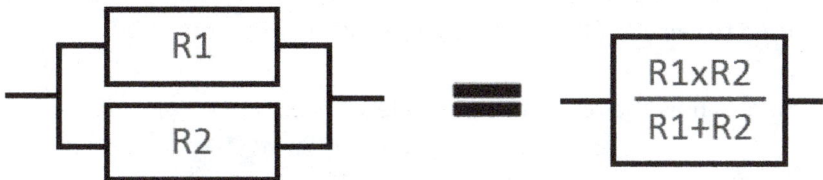

Web Address

http://www.101computing.net/resistor-in-series-and-parallel/

Python Code

```python
1.  #Resistors in series and parallel -
    www.101computing.net/resistor-in-series-and-parallel/
2.
3.  print("**********************************")
4.  print("*                                *")
5.  print("*  Resistors in Series or Parallel  *")
6.  print("*                                *")
7.  print("**********************************")
8.
9.  #INPUT - Retrieve User Input
10. r1 = int(input("Value of Resistor 1?"))
11. r2 = int(input("Value of Resistor 2?"))
12.
13. option=input("Series or Parallel?").lower()
14. while option!="series" and option!="parallel":
15.   print("Sorry this is not valid option - Try again:")
16.   option = input("Series or Parallel?").lower()
17.
18. #PROCESS: Calculate Total Resistance
19. if option=="series":
20.   r = r1 + r2
21. elif option=="parallel":
22.   r = int((r1*r2) / (r1+r2))
23.
24. #OUTPUT - Display Total Resistance on screen
25. print("The total resistance is " + str(r) + " Ohms.")
```

16. Resistor Value Calculator

When designing electronic circuits you may need to use resistors. Each resistor has a resistance value expressed in ohms (Ω). Resistors are identified by a series of concentric coloured bands. Each band colour has a value which is used to calculate the resistance value of the resistor.

Here is how the resistor colour code works:

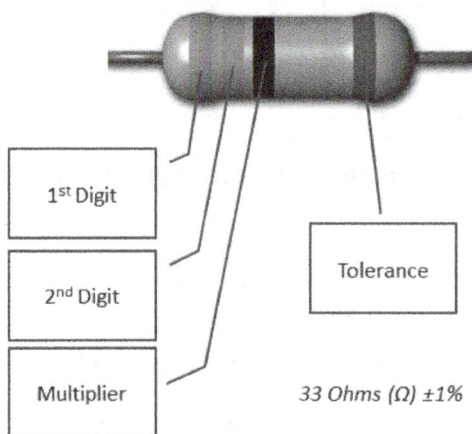

1st Digit

2nd Digit

Multiplier

Tolerance

33 Ohms (Ω) ±1%

Colour	1st Digit	2nd Digit	Multiplier	Tolerance
Black	0	0	x 1	
Brown	1	1	x 10	±1%
Red	2	2	x 100	±2%
Orange	3	3	x 1,000	
Yellow	4	4	x 10,000	
Green	5	5	x 100,000	±0.5%
Blue	6	6	x 1,000,000	±0.25%
Violet	7	7	x 10,000,000	±0.1%
Grey	8	8		±0.05%
White	9	9		
Gold				±5%
Silver				±10%

This challenge consists of writing a program that asks the user to enter three colours (e.g. Red, Red, Green) and returns the resistance value (e.g. 2,200,000 Ω or 2,200 kΩ).

Web Address

http://www.101computing.net/resistor-value-calculator/

Python Code

```
1.  #Resistor Value Calculator -
      http://www.101computing.net/resistor-value-calculator/
2.
3.  def getColourValue(colour):
4.    if colour=="black":
5.      return 0
6.    elif colour=="brown":
7.      return 1
8.    elif colour=="red":
9.      return 2
10.   elif colour=="orange":
11.     return 3
12.   elif colour=="yellow":
13.     return 4
14.   elif colour=="green":
15.     return 5
16.   elif colour=="blue":
17.     return 6
18.   elif colour=="violet":
19.     return 7
20.   elif colour=="grey":
21.     return 8
22.   elif colour=="white":
23.     return 9
24.
25. #Retrieving User inputs
26. colour1 = input("what colour is the first ring?").lower()
27. colour2 = input("what colour is the second ring?").lower()
28. colour3 = input("what colour is the third ring?").lower()
29.
30. #Workout resistance value
31. resistance = str(getColourValue(colour1)) + str(getColourVal
      ue(colour2)) + str(getColourValue(colour3) * "0")
32.
33. #Output resistance value on screen
34. print("Total resistance: " + resistance + " ohms.")
```

17. Poker Dice Game

The aim of this challenge is to create a simplified game of Poker Dice using only three dice.
The computer will generate three random numbers between one and six and the user will score points as follows:

- Three of a kind: +50pts
- Straight (e.g. 3,4,5): +30pts
- Three odd numbers: +15pts
- Three even numbers: +15pts
- One pair: +10pts

Web Address

http://www.101computing.net/fancy-a-game-of-poker-dice/

Python Code

```
1.  #Poker Dice Challenge - www.101computing.net/fancy-a-game-
    of-poker-dice/
2.  from random import randint
3.
4.  def isEven(number):
5.      if (number % 2 == 0):
6.          return True
7.      else:
8.          return False
9.
10. def isOdd(number):
11.     if (number % 2 == 1):
12.         return True
13.     else:
14.         return False
15.
16. #My Program starts here
17. print("### Poker Dice ####")
18. print("")
19.
20. #Throwing the three dice:
21. dice1=randint(1,6)
22. dice2=randint(1,6)
23. dice3=randint(1,6)
```

```
24. print("Dice 1: " + str(dice1))
25. print("Dice 2: " + str(dice2))
26. print("Dice 3: " + str(dice3))
27. print("")
28.
29. score=0
30.
31. #Check if we have 3 even numbers
32. if isEven(dice1)==True and isEven(dice2)==True and isEven(di
    ce3)==True:
33.     print("3 Even Numbers!")
34.     score = score + 15
35.
36. #Check if we have 3 odd numbers
37. if isOdd(dice1)==True and isOdd(dice2)==True and isOdd(dice3
    )==True:
38.     print("3 Odd Numbers!")
39.     score = score + 15
40.
41. #Check if we have 3 of a kind
42. if dice1==dice2 and dice1==dice3:
43.     print("3 Of A Kind!")
44.     score = score + 50
45. else:
46.   #Check if we have a pair
47.   if dice1==dice2 or dice2==dice3 or dice1==dice3:
48.     print("A Pair!")
49.     score = score + 10
50.
51. #Check if we have a straight
52. if (dice1-dice2)==1 and (dice2-dice3)==1:
53.   score = score + 30
54. if (dice1-dice3)==1 and (dice3-dice2)==1:
55.   score = score + 30
56. if (dice3-dice2)==1 and (dice2-dice1)==1:
57.   score = score + 30
58. if (dice3-dice1)==1 and (dice1-dice2)==1:
59.   score = score + 30
60. if (dice2-dice3)==1 and (dice3-dice1)==1:
61.   score = score + 30
62. if (dice2-dice1)==1 and (dice2-dice3)==1:
63.   score = score + 30
64.
65. #Display Final Score:
66. print("Your score is: " + str(score) + " points")
```

Chapter #3: Loop the loop

Sequencing and Selection are two extremely useful programming constructs that help us build very complex programs.

While completing some of the previous challenges you may have been tempted to repeat some lines of code to allow the user to play the program several times without having to restart it.

This can be done using **iteration**. This programming construct allows a section of code to be repeated several times using a loop. A loop acts similarly to an IF statement but, instead of allowing the computer to jump downwards within the code (to bypass code when a condition is not met), a loop allows the computer to jump upwards to a line of code that has already been executed previously. This allows a section of code to be repeated, either a fixed number of times (**Count-controlled *For* loop**) or until a condition is met (**Condition-controlled *While* loop**).

In the next few challenges we will be using:

- Iteration using Count-Controlled Loops (*For* loops),
- Iteration using Condition-Controlled Loops (*While* loops),
- Nested Loops,
- Nested Loops and IF Statements.

18. Live Metrics

Before starting this challenge we invite you to visit the following two web pages used to display dynamic statistics on different topics including the number of posts on various social networks and blogging platforms:
- http://www.internetlivestats.com/
- http://www.worldometers.info/

In this challenge we are going to write our own Python script to generate live metrics based on the following information:

> *Every second, on average 6,000 tweets are tweeted on Twitter.*

> *On average 2,430,310 emails are sent worldwide every second.*

> *Google now processes over 40,000 search queries every second on average.*

> *Around 60 million cars are produced in a single year worldwide.*

Web Address

http://www.101computing.net/live-metrics/

Python Code

```
1.  #Live Metrics Challenge - www.101computing.net/live-
    metrics
2.  import time
3.
4.  #Initialise variables
5.  numberOfTweets = 0
6.  numberOfEmails = 0
7.  numberOfGoogleSearches = 0
8.  numberOfCars = 0
9.  worldPopulation = 7370000000
10.
11. #Repeat every 1 second:
12. while True:
13.   time.sleep(1)
14.   #Every second, on average, around 6,000 tweets are tweeted
      on Twitter
15.   numberOfTweets += 6000
16.   print("Since you started this program " + str(numberOfTwee
      ts) + " tweets have been tweeted on Twitter")
17.
18.   #Every second, on average, around 2,430,310 emails are sen
      t worldwide
19.   numberOfEmails += 2430310
20.   print("Since you started this program " + str(numberOfEmai
      ls) + " emails have been sent.")
21.
22.   #Every second, on average, around 40,000 google search que
      ries
23.   numberOfGoogleSearches += 40000
24.   print("Since you started this program " + str(numberOfGoog
      leSearches) + " Google searches have been requested.")
25.
26.   #Every year 60 millions cars are sold aroung the world
27.   #Calculate number of cars sold per seconds
```

```
28.  numberOfCars += 60000000/(365*24*60*60)
29.  print("Since you started this program " + str(int(numberOf
     Cars)) + " cars have been sold around the world.")
30.
31.  #The world population is currently growing at a rate of ar
     ound 1.13 % per year.
32.  worldPopulation += worldPopulation * (1.13 / 100) / (365 *
     24 *60 *60)
33.  print("World Population: " + str(int(worldPopulation)))
```

19. Fizz-Buzz Game

Fizz buzz is a group word game for children to teach
them about division. Players take turns to count
incrementally, replacing any number divisible by three
with the word "fizz", and any number divisible by five with the word
"buzz".

For this challenge you need to write a computer program that will display
all the numbers between 1 and 100.

- For each number divisible by three the computer will display the
  word "fizz",
- For each number divisible by five the computer will display the
  word "buzz",
- For each number divisible by three and by five the computer will
  display the word "fizz-buzz",

This is what the output will look like:

1 - 2 - Fizz - 4 - Buzz - Fizz - 7 ...

Tip:
To find out if a number can be divided by another number, you will need
to check the remainder of the division by using the % sign in Python. For
instance:

- 7 % 3 = 1 because 7 is not divisible by 3.
- 6 % 3 = 0 because 6 is divisible by 3.

So to check if number1 can be divided by number2, you can check if: number1 % number2 == 0.

Web Address
http://www.101computing.net/fizz-buzz-game/

Python Code

```
1.  #Fizz-Buzz Challenge - www.101computing.net/fizz-buzz-
    game/
2.
3.  for number in range(1,101):
4.    if number % 3 == 0 and number % 5 == 0:
5.      print("Fizz-Buzz!")
6.    elif number % 3 == 0:
7.      print("Fizz!")
8.    elif number % 5 == 0:
9.      print("Buzz!")
10.   else:
11.     print number
```

20. The legend of the chessboard

The story tells us that long long ago the great Sultan of India loved to play games. As he started to get bored of the games that were present at the time he asked a wise man who lived in his kingdom to come up with a new game.

This, according to the legend, is how the game of chess was invented. The Sultan was very pleased with the wise man who had invented the game and in return he offered the wise man a reward of his own choosing. To the Sultan's surprise, the wise man did not ask for any gold. Instead he only had one request: he asked just for a few grains of rice in the following manner: the sultan was to put a single grain of rice on the first chess square, two grains on the second square, four on the third square and carry on doubling this number on every consequent square to fill up all 64 squares of the chessboard. This seemed to the ruler to be a modest request, so he called for his servants to bring the rice. Did the Sultan manage to fulfil the wise man's request?

Your task consists of writing a python script to calculate the total number of grains of rice required to cover the chessboard following's the wise man's request.

Web Address

http://www.101computing.net/the-legend-of-the-chessboard/

Python Code

```
1.  #The legend of the chessboard - www.101computing.net/the-
    legend-of-the-chessboard/
2.
3.  #Initialise Variables
4.  riceTotal = 0
5.  riceOnCell = 1
6.
7.  #Repeat calculation over the 64 cells of the chessboard
8.  for i in range(0,64):
9.      riceTotal += riceOnCell
10.     riceOnCell = riceOnCell * 2
11.
12. #Output result
13. print("Total number of grains of rice:")
14. print(riceOnCell)
```

21. Times Table Challenge

Our aim is to write a program to display the full times table in a grid with operands ranging from 1 to 10.

To do so we will use nested "for loops" to calculate and display all 100 values of this times table.

Our code will also ensure that all numbers are properly lined up which can be tricky as some of the values are one digit long (numbers 0 to 9) whereas other values are two digits long (numbers 10 to 99) or even three digits long (number 100).

Times Table										
X	1	2	3	4	5	6	7	8	9	10
1	1	2	3	4	5	6	7	8	9	10
2	2	4	6	8	10	12	14	16	18	20
3	3	6	9	12	15	18	21	24	27	30
4	4	8	12	16	20	24	28	32	36	40
5	5	10	15	20	25	30	35	40	45	50
6	6	12	18	24	30	36	42	48	54	60
7	7	14	21	28	35	42	49	56	63	70
8	8	16	24	32	40	48	56	64	72	80
9	9	18	27	36	45	54	63	72	81	90
10	10	20	30	40	50	60	70	80	90	100

Web Address

http://www.101computing.net/times-table-challenge/

Python Code

```
1.  #Times table Challenge - www.101computing.net/times-table-
    challenge/
2.
3.  print(" --- 10 x 10 Times Table --- ")
4.  print("")
5.  print("X | 1  2  3  4  5  6  7  8  9  10")
6.  print("--+----------------------------")
7.
8.  # 10 lines/rows
9.  for i in range (1,11):
10.   if i < 10:
11.     line = str(i) + " |"
12.   else:
13.     line = str(i) + "|"
14.
15.   # 10 Columns
16.   for j in range (1,11):
17.     value = i*j
18.     if value < 10:
19.       line = line + " " + str(value) + " "
20.     else:
21.       line = line + " " + str(value)
22.   print(line)
```

22. Prime Numbers

A prime number is a number that can be divided evenly only by 1, or itself. A prime number must be a whole number greater than 1.

2, 3, 5, 7, 11, 13, 17... are all examples of prime numbers.

Our challenge is to write a program that will list all the prime numbers between 1 and 1000.

Web Address

http://www.101computing.net/prime-number-check-in-python/

Python Code

```
1.  #Prime Numbers List - www.101computing.net/prime-number-
    check-in-python/
2.
3.  #A function to check if a number is a prime number or not
4.  def isPrime(number):
5.      prime=True
6.      for i in range(2,number):
7.          if number % i ==0:
8.              prime=False
9.              break
10.     return prime
11.
12. print("Prime numbers between 1 and 999:")
13. for i in range(2,1000):
14.     if isPrime(i):
15.         print(i)
```

23. The Collatz Conjecture

The Collatz conjecture is a famous mathematical mystery that has yet to be solved. It is named after Lothar Collatz a German mathematician, who first proposed it in 1937. It is based on the following number sequence:

1. Start with any positive whole number called n,
2. if n is even, divide it by 2: n' = n / 2,
3. if n is odd, multiply it by 3 and add 1: n' = 3 x n + 1,
4. if n' = 1 then stop the number sequence,
5. otherwise repeat this process with n' as your starting number.

Let's see how this number sequence behaves with some of the following numbers:

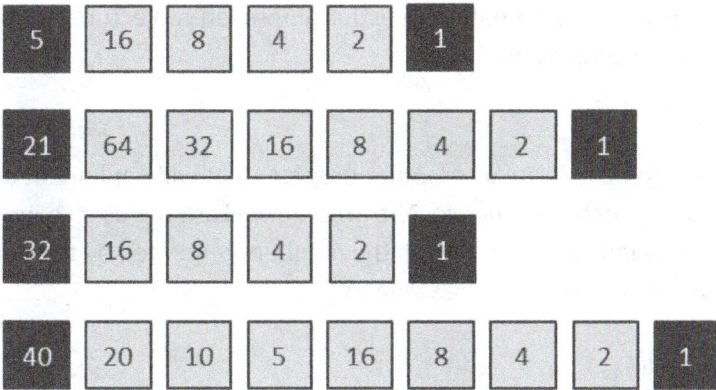

| 5 | 16 | 8 | 4 | 2 | 1 |

| 21 | 64 | 32 | 16 | 8 | 4 | 2 | 1 |

| 32 | 16 | 8 | 4 | 2 | 1 |

| 40 | 20 | 10 | 5 | 16 | 8 | 4 | 2 | 1 |

Collatz-Conjoncture

These number sequences are known as hailstone sequences because they go up and down just like a hailstone in a cloud before crashing to Earth. It seems that these sequences always end up reaching an endless cycle: the endless cycle being 4, 2 , 1. (If we carry on, 1 being odd becomes 3 x 1 + 1 = 4).

... | 4 | 2 | 1 | 4 | 2 | 1 | 4 | 2 | 1 | ...

An unsolved problem:

The question that these sequences are raising is: do such number sequences always settle on the 4,2,1 cycle no matter what starting value we use? It is conjectured (but not yet proven) that they will, in other words that each hailstone sequence will always terminate at n = 1.

Experiments certainly suggest that it does. Computers have checked all starting values up to 5×2^{60}, a number that is 19 digits long, and found that the 4, 2, 1 cycle eventually appears. The trouble is that nobody has been able to prove that this is the case for all starting numbers!

This unsolved mathematical question/unproven conjecture is known as the **Collatz conjecture**.

Our Challenge

We are going to write a computer program that will implement a hailstone number sequence. The program will ask the user to input the starting number and display all the numbers generated by the number sequence till it reaches the value of 1.

Web Address

http://www.101computing.net/the-collatz-conjecture/

Python Code

```
1.  # Hailstone Number Sequence - www.101computing.net/the-
    collatz-conjecture/
2.
3.  #A function to find out if a number is an odd number
4.  def isOdd(number):
5.    if number % 2 == 1:
6.      return True
7.    else:
8.      return False
9.
10. n = int(input("Type a positive whole number to start your ha
    ilstone sequence:"))
11.
12. print(">>> Hailstone Number Sequence: n = " + str(n))
13. while n!=1:
```

```
14.    if isOdd(n):
15.       #n is Odd
16.       n = 3 * n +1
17.    else:
18.       # n is even
19.       n = n / 2
20.    print(int(n))
```

24. Calculating Pi

Pi (π) is one of the most important and fascinating
numbers in mathematics. Roughly 3.14, it is a constant
that is used to calculate the circumference of a circle
from that circle's radius or diameter. Pi is also an irrational number, which
means that it can be calculated to an infinite number of decimal places
without ever slipping into a repeating pattern. This makes it difficult, but
not impossible, to calculate precisely.

How to calculate Pi?

Method #1: Pi = Circumference / Diameter
All we need to calculate Pi is a round object such as a golf ball and a tape
measurer. We will need to take two measurements: the diameter and the
circumference of the sphere/object.

Knowing that Circumference = π x Diameter we can calculate π as follows:
π = Circumference / Diameter.

	Diameter	Diameter of a golf ball: *4.27 cm*
	Circumference	Circumference of a golf ball: *13.41 cm*
π		Pi = Circumference / Diameter *13.411 / 4.267* $\overset{\sim}{=}$ *3.1405*

As you may have noticed, this method does not give you the exact value of Pi. This is due to the fact that the measurements of the diameter and of the circumference of an object are never 100% accurate.

Method #2: Calculating Pi Using an Infinite Series (Gregory-Leibniz series)

Mathematicians have found several different mathematical series that, if carried out infinitely, will accurately calculate Pi to a great number of decimal places. Some of these are so complex they require supercomputers to process them. One of the simplest, however, is the Gregory-Leibniz series. Though not very efficient, it will get closer and closer to Pi with every iteration, accurately producing Pi to five decimal places with 500,000 iterations. Here is the formula to apply:

$$\pi = 4/1 - 4/3 + 4/5 -$$
$$4/7 + 4/9 - 4/11 + 4/13$$
$$- 4/15 + 4/17 - 4/19 \ldots$$

Method #3: Calculating Pi Using an Infinite Series (Nilakantha series)

The Nilakantha series is another infinite series to calculate Pi that is fairly easy to understand. While somewhat more complicated, it converges on Pi much quicker than the Gregory-Leibniz formula. Here is the formula to apply:

$$\pi = 3 + 4/(2\text{x}3\text{x}4)$$
$$- 4/(4\text{x}5\text{x}6) + 4/(6\text{x}7\text{x}8)$$
$$- 4/(8\text{x}9\text{x}10) + 4/(10\text{x}11\text{x}12)$$
$$- \ldots$$

Our challenge consists of writing a Python program that will estimate the value of Pi using each of the three methods described above.

Web Address

http://www.101computing.net/calculating-pi/

Python Code

```
1.  #Calculating Pi using a Python Script: www.101computing.net/
    calculating-pi
2.
```

```
3.  print("--------- Caluclating Pi ---------")
4.  print("")
5.  print(" 1. Using Pi = Circumference / Diameter formula")
6.  print(" 2. Using the Gregory-Leibniz series")
7.  print(" 3. Using the Nilakantha series")
8.  print("")
9.  option = input("Which method would like to use (1,2 or 3)?")

10.
11. if option=="1":
12.   #Using Pi = Circumference / Diameter formula
13.   circumference = float(input("Enter the circumference of yo
      ur sphere:"))
14.   diameter = float(input("Enter the diameter of your sphere:
      "))
15.   pi = circumference / diameter
16.   print("Estimated Pi = " + str(pi))
17.
18. elif option=="2":
19.   #Using the Gregory-Leibniz series
20.   iteration = int(input("Enter the number of iterations (e.g
      . 5000)"))
21.   pi = 0
22.   sign = 1
23.   for i in range(0, iteration):
24.     denominator = 1 + 2*i
25.     pi += sign * 4/denominator
26.     sign = sign * (-1)
27.   print("Estimated Pi = " + str(pi))
28.
29. elif option=="3":
30.   #Using the Nilakantha series
31.   iteration = int(input("Enter the number of iterations (e.g
      . 5000)"))
32.   pi = 3
33.   sign = 1
34.   for i in range(1, iteration+1):
35.     denominator = (2*i) * (2*i+1) * (2*i+2)
36.     pi += sign * 4/denominator
37.     sign = sign * (-1)
38.   print("Estimated Pi = " + str(pi))
39.
40. else:
41.   print("Not a valid option.")
```

25. Binary Converter

Everything that is stored on a computer is stored as binary code. Binary code is made of bits (0 or 1). We often use Bytes to store data. A Byte is made of eight bits and can be used to store any whole number between 0 and 255. The conversion table below is used to convert a binary number into a denary number.

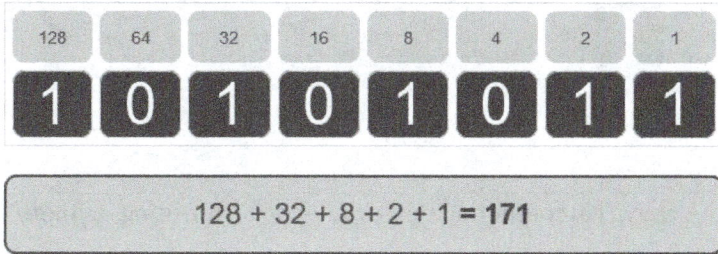

128	64	32	16	8	4	2	1
1	0	1	0	1	0	1	1

128 + 32 + 8 + 2 + 1 = **171**

The purpose of this challenge is to write a Python script to convert a Binary number into denary and vice versa. To do so we will use the concept of binary left and right shifts as explained below.

Binary Left Shift

A binary left shift is used to multiply a binary number by two. It consists of shifting all the binary digits to the left by one digit and adding an extra digit at the end with a value of 0.

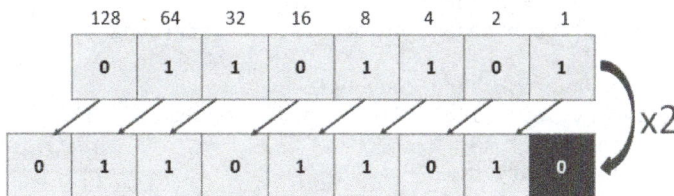

128	64	32	16	8	4	2	1
0	1	1	0	1	1	0	1

0	1	1	0	1	1	0	1	0

x2

Binary Right Shift

A binary right shift is used to divide a binary number by two. It consists of shifting all the binary digits to the right by one digit and adding an extra digit at the beginning (to the left) with a value of 0.

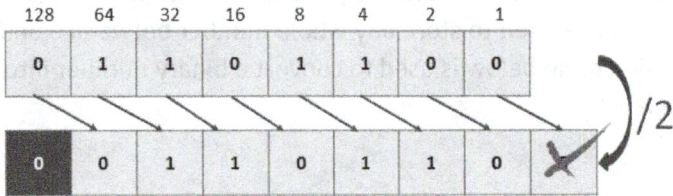

Web Address

http://www.101computing.net/binary-converter-using -python/

Practise your binary conversions

http://www.101computing.net/binary-converter/

Python Code

```
1.  #Binary Converter - www.101computing.net/binary-converter-
    using-python/
2.
3.  #Binary to denary conversion
4.  binary = input("Input a number in binary:")
5.  denary = 0
6.  for digit in binary:
7.    #A left shift in binary means x2
8.    denary = denary*2 + int(digit)
9.  print("Your denary number is: " + str(denary))
10.
11. #Denary to binary conversion
12. denary = int(input("Input a denary number:"))
13. binary=""
14. while denary>0:
15.   #A left shift in binary means /2
16.   binary = str(denary%2) + binary
17.   denary = denary//2
18. print("Your binary number is: " + binary)
```

26. Fraction Simplifier

This challenge consists of writing a program that asks the end-user to enter a fraction (numerator and denominator) and output the matching reduced fraction when the fraction can be reduced.

$$\frac{numerator}{denominator}$$

To simplify a fraction your program will need to find the greatest common divisor (aka greatest common factor) of the numerator and denominator that will have been entered by the end-user. Then, your program will divide the numerator and denominator of the fraction by this number.

$$\frac{9}{24} = \frac{3x3}{8x3} = \frac{3}{8}$$

To find out if a number is a factor of the numerator you will need to check that the remainder of the numerator divided by this number is null (=0).

For instance 3 is a factor of 24 because 24 mod 3 = 0.

$$24 = 8 \times 3 + \underline{0}$$

$$24 \bmod 3 = \underline{0}$$

The remainder of 24 divided by 3 is 0

In Python:
$$24\%3 = \underline{0}$$

Whereas 5 is NOT a factor of 32 because 32 mod 5 = 2 != 0.

$$32 = 6 \times 5 + \underline{2}$$

$$32 \bmod 5 = \underline{2}$$

The remainder of 32 divided by 5 is 2

In Python:
$$32\%5 = \underline{2}$$

http://www.101computing.net/fraction-simplifier/

Python Code

```
1.  #Fraction Simplifier Challenge -
    www.101computing.net/fraction-simplifier/
2.
3.  print("####### Fraction Simplifier #######\n\n")
4.  numerator = int(input("Enter the numerator:"))
5.  denominator = int(input("Enter the denominator:"))
6.
7.  print("\nYour fraction is: " + str(numerator) + "/" + str(de
    nominator))
8.
9.  print("\nLet's try to simplify this fraction.")
10.
11. if numerator>=denominator:
12.   upperBound = numerator
13. else:
14.   upperBound = denominator
15.
16. for i in range(upperBound, 1, -1):
17.   if numerator%i == 0 and denominator%i == 0:
18.     numerator = numerator // i
19.     denominator = denominator // i
20.
21. print("\nYour simplified fraction is: " + str(numerator) + "
    /" + str(denominator))
```

27. Check Digit Validation

A barcode is an optical, representation of data that can easily be scanned by a barcode reader.

A barcode is used to store a number such as the product code of a product for sale in a shop, or the ISBN number of a book. The barcode you scan in a shop most likely uses the UPC-A (Universal Product Code) format which means that it consists of 12 numerical digits (0 to 9).

0 36000 29145 2

With a UPC barcode, the last digit is called the check digit. The check digit is used to make sure a barcode has been entered (typed) or scanned correctly to minimise human errors or scanning errors.

The check digit is a result of a complex calculation based on the 11 first digits of the barcode. Every time a barcode is scanned, the computer completes this calculation again using the first 11 digits to calculate the check digit. It then compares this with the 12th digit of the barcode. If these two are the same, the barcode scanned is most likely valid. If they are different the scanner will beep to indicate that the barcode was not scanned properly.

The check digit is a fairly complex calculation that is performed in 3 steps as follows:

1. Add the digits in the odd-numbered positions (first, third, fifth, etc.) together and multiply by three.
2. Add the digits (up to but not including the check digit) in the even-numbered positions (second, fourth, sixth, etc.) to the result.
3. Take the remainder of the result divided by 10 (modulo operation) and if not 0, subtract this from 10 to derive the check digit.

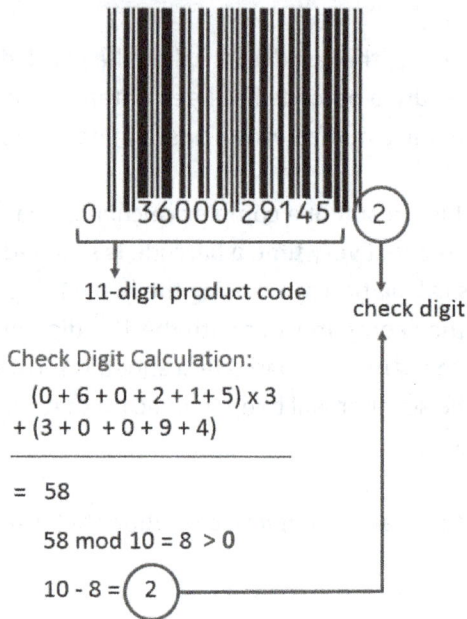

11-digit product code   check digit

Check Digit Calculation:

$(0 + 6 + 0 + 2 + 1+ 5) \times 3$
$+ (3 + 0 + 0 + 9 + 4)$

$= 58$

$58 \bmod 10 = 8 > 0$

$10 - 8 = (2)$

Our challenge consists of writing a Python program that will receive a 12-digit UPC-A barcode (11 digits + 1 check digit). Our Python script will then calculate the expected check digit matching the 11-digit product code. If this calculated check digit matches the 12th digit of the barcode, our program will output a "Valid barcode" message, if not it will output an "Invalid barcode" message.

Web Address

http://www.101computing.net/upc-barcode-check-digit-calculation/

Python Code

```
1. #Check Digit Validation - www.101computing.net/upc-barcode-
   check-digit-calculation/
2.
3. barcode = input("Enter 12-digit UPC-A barcode:")
4. while len(barcode)!=12:
5.     print("Invalid UPC-A barcode.")
6.     barcode = input("Re-enter 12-digit UPC-A barcode:")
7.
8. checkDigit = int(barcode[11]) #12th digit
9. print("Check digit: " + str(checkDigit))
```

```
10.
11. #Calculate check digit
12. oddDigits = int(barcode[0]) + int(barcode[2]) + int(barcode[
    4]) + int(barcode[6]) + int(barcode[8]) + int(barcode[10])
13. evenDigits = int(barcode[1]) + int(barcode[3]) + int(barcode
    [5]) + int(barcode[7]) + int(barcode[9])
14. total = oddDigits * 3 + evenDigits
15. remainder = total % 10
16. if remainder == 0:
17.   calculatedCheckDigit = 0
18. else:
19.   calculatedCheckDigit = 10 - remainder
20.
21. print("Calculated Check Digit: " + str(calculatedCheckDigit)
    )
22.
23. #Compare both check digits to see if the barcode is valid
24. if checkDigit == calculatedCheckDigit:
25.   print("Valid Barcode")
26. else:
27.   print("Invalid Barcode")
```

28. Sweet Shop

Have you ever been in a sweet shop to buy sweets?
For this challenge we are going to spend £5 in a sweet
shop hence we need to find out how many sweets we
can afford. We will want to pick and mix sweets until we have spent all
our money.

To help us buy our sweets we are going
to write a program that will help us
decide how many sweets we can afford
while allowing us to pick and mix
different types of sweets.

Here are the main steps of our program
which will:

--- Price List ---

A - Marshmallow: £0.20
B - Bubble gum: £0.30
C - Jelly Bean: £0.15
D - Candy Stick: £0.35
E - Cola Whips: £0.22

X - Exit

1. Display a price list of all the sweets available in the shop,
2. Ask the end-user how much they would like to spend,
3. Ask the user which sweet they would like to buy and how many of them they would like (A to E),
4. Allow the user to enter X (instead of the A to E letter for a sweet) to stop buying more sweets,
5. Check whether the user can afford these sweets and if they can, calculate and display how much money they have left,
6. Repeat steps 3 to 5 for as long as the user has some money left.

Web Address

http://www.101computing.net/sweet-shop/

Python Code

```
1.  #Sweet Shop Challenge - www.101computing.net/sweet-shop/
2.
3.  print(" --- Price List --- ")
4.  print("")
5.  print("A -  Marshmallow: $0.20")
6.  print("B -  Bubble gum: $0.30")
7.  print("C -  Jelly Bean: $0.15")
8.  print("D -  Candy Stick: $0.35")
9.  print("E -  Cola Whips: $0.22")
10. print("")
11. print("X - Exit")
12. print("")
13. money = float(input("How much do you want to spend?"))
14.
15. while money > 0:
16.     sweet = input("Which sweets do you want to buy  (Type a
        letter from A to E or X to exit).?")
17.     if sweet == "X":
18.        print("No more sweets required.")
19.        break
20.     quantity = int(input("How many of these do you want to b
        uy?"))
21.     cost = 0
22.
23.     if sweet == "A":
24.        cost = 0.20 * quantity
25.     elif sweet == "B":
26.        cost = 0.30 * quantity
27.     elif sweet == "C":
```

```
28.          cost = 0.15 * quantity
29.      elif sweet == "D":
30.          cost = 0.35 * quantity
31.      elif sweet == "E":
32.          cost = 0.22 * quantity
33.
34.      #Can the user afford this?
35.      if money >= cost:
36.          money = money - cost
37.      else:
38.          print("You do not have enough money for this quantity!
    ")
39.
40.      print("Money left: " + str(money))
41.
42. print("Good Bye!")
```

29. Fruit Machine

In this challenge we will complete a full Python Program to simulate a fruit machine. We will use the random library to randomly select and display three pieces of fruit on screen. We will use if statements to check if the user has won the Jackpot!

Web Address

http://www.101computing.net/fruit-machine/

Python Code

```
1.  #Fruit Machine - www.101Computing.net/fruit-machine
2.
3.  import random
4.
5.  print("############################")
6.  print("#                          #")
7.  print("#        Fruit Machine      #")
8.  print("#                          #")
9.  print("############################")
10. print("")
11.
12. wheel = ["Banana","Apple","Cherry","Pear"]
```

```
13.
14. while True:
15.     play = input("Press enter to start the fruit machine or
    X to exit").upper()
16.
17.     if play=="X":
18.         break;
19.
20.     print("\n *** Spinning Wheels... *** \n")
21.
22.     fruit1 = random.choice(wheel)
23.     fruit2 = random.choice(wheel)
24.     fruit3 = random.choice(wheel)
25.
26.     print(" === " + fruit1 + " - " + fruit2 + " -
    " + fruit3 + " ===\n")
27.
28.     if fruit1 == fruit2 == fruit3:
29.         print(" $$$ Jackpot! $$$\n")
30.     elif fruit1 == fruit3:
31.         print(" $-$ Split! $-$\n")
32.     else:
33.         print(" :-( Unlucky... have another go!\n")
34.
35. print ("\n\n >>> Good Bye <<<")
```

30. Penalty Shootout

For this challenge we are going to write a computer program where the user tries to score a goal against the computer.

The user will be asked where they want to shoot and will have to choose one of the following five options:
- TL: Top Left,
- BL: Bottom Left,
- M: Middle,
- TR: Top Right,
- BR: Bottom Right.

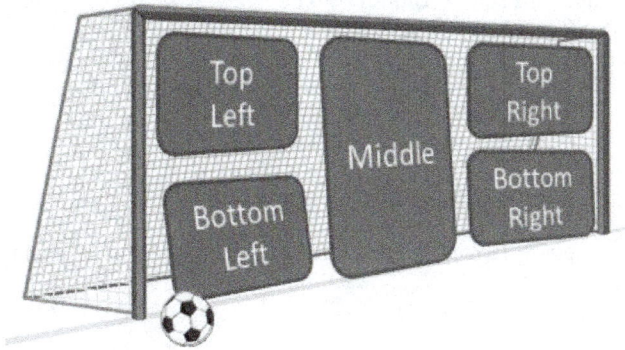

The computer will act as the goal keeper and randomly choose one of these options too.

The program will decide if there is a goal or not by comparing the user's choice with the computer option.

Web Address

http://www.101computing.net/penalty-shootout/

Python Code

```
1.  #Penalty Shootout - www.101computing.net/penalty-shootout/
2.  import random
3.
4.  print("    _____    ")
5.  print("    |                     |    ")
6.  print("    |                     |    ")
7.  print("    |   Penalty Shootout  |    ")
8.  print("    |                     |    ")
9.  print("____|_____|____")
10. print("")
11. print("")
12.
13. score = 0
14. for counter in range (1,6):
15.     #Let the computer decides where it wants the goal to dive

16.     options=["TL","BL","M","TR","BR"]
17.     computerOption = random.choice(options)
18.
19.     #Now let's ask the user where they want to shoot
```

```
20.    userOption = input("Where do you want to shoot? (TL, BL,
       M, TR or BR)")
21.
22.    #Then we can check if the goal blocked the ball or not
23.    if userOption == computerOption:
24.      print("The goal blocked it!")
25.    else:
26.      print("You scored a goal!")
27.      score = score + 1
28.      print("Your score so far is: " + str(score))
29.
30. print("Game Over")
```

31. Rock Paper Scissors

Rock-paper-scissors is a hand game usually played by two people, where players simultaneously form one of three shapes with an outstretched hand. The "rock" beats scissors, the "scissors" beat paper and the "paper" beats rock; if both players throw the same shape, the game is tied.

Web Address

http://www.101computing.net/rock-paper-scissors/

Python Code

```
1.   #Rock Paper Scissors - www.101computing.net/rock-paper-
     scissors/
2.   import random
3.
4.   #Initialise the game
5.   options=["rock","paper","scissors"]
6.   userScore=0
7.   computerScore=0
8.
9.   while True:
10.    userOption = input("Rock, Paper or Scissors?").lower()
11.    computerOption = random.choice(options)
12.
13.    print("You said: " + userOption)
14.    print("The computer chose: " + computerOption)
15.
16.    if (userOption==computerOption):
```

```
17.        print("It's a draw...")
18.    elif ((userOption=="rock") and (computerOption=="scissors"
       )):
19.        print("You win!")
20.        userScore = userScore + 1
21.    elif ((userOption=="paper") and (computerOption=="rock")):

22.        print("You win!")
23.        userScore = userScore + 1
24.    elif ((userOption=="scissors") and (computerOption=="paper
       ")):
25.        print("You win!")
26.        userScore = userScore + 1
27.    else:
28.        print("You lose!")
29.        computerScore = computerScore + 1
30.
31.    if (computerScore==3) or (userScore==3):
32.        break
33.
34. #End of Game - And th efinal winner is...
35. if (userScore>computerScore):
36.    print("You win with a score of " + str(userScore) + " agai
       nst " + str(computerScore))
37. elif (userScore<computerScore):
38.    print("The computer wins with a score of " + str(computerS
       core) + " against " + str(userScore))
39. else:
40.    print("It's a draw " + str(userScore) + " against " + str(
       computerScore))
```

32. What's My Change?

For this challenge we will write a program that
prompts the end-user to enter two values:

- Value 1: amount to be paid by the customer,
- Value 2: amount received from the customer.

The program should then find out how many banknotes or coins of
different values should be returned. It will accept banknotes of £20, £10
and £5 and the following coins: £2, £1, 50p, 20p, 10p, 5p, 2p, 1p.

Python Code

```python
1.  #What's my change - www.101computing.net/whats-my-change/
2.
3.  amountDue = float(input("Amount to be paid?"))
4.  amountReceived = float(input("Amount received?"))
5.
6.  if amountReceived<amountDue:
7.    print("Not enough money  from customer!")
8.  else:
9.    change = amountReceived - amountDue
10.   print("Your Change: £" + str(change))
11.   values=[20,10,5,2,1,0.5,0.2,0.1,0.05,0.02,0.01]
12.   for value in values:
13.     if change>=value:
14.       total = int(change // value)
15.       if value>=5:
16.         print(str(total) + " x £" + str(value) + " banknote(
    s)")
17.       elif value>=1:
18.         print(str(total) + " x £" + str(value) + " coin(s)")
19.       else:
20.         print(str(total) + " x " + str(int(value * 100)) + "
    pence coin(s)")
21.       change = change - total * value
22.
23. print("The End.")
```

33. My Arithmetic Quiz

For this challenge we will create a maths quiz
consisting of ten arithmetic questions. Each question
will be randomly generated using two random
operands between 1 and 12 and one random operator, either + (addition),
- (subtraction) or x (multiplication). We will not include the division
operator as this could result in a decimal value.

We will include a scoring system to our quiz. The player will be asked one question at a time and score 10 points per correct answer and lose 5 points per incorrect answer.

Web Address

http://www.101computing.net/arithmetic-quiz/

Python Code

```
1.  #Arithmetic Quiz Challenge -
    www.101computing.net/arithmetic-quiz
2.  import random
3.
4.  #A function to validate the user input and only accept whole
    numbers
5.  def inputNumber(message):
6.    while True:
7.      try:
8.        userInput = int(input(message))
9.      except ValueError:
10.       print("Not an integer! Try again.")
11.       continue
12.     else:
13.       return userInput
14.       break
15.
16. print("+-x+-x+-x+-x+-x+-x+-x+-x+-x+-x+")
17. print("+      Arithmetic Quiz        +")
18. print("+-x+-x+-x+-x+-x+-x+-x+-x+-x+-x+")
19.
20. #Display Instructions
21. print("Answers the following 10 questions...")
22.
23. #Initialise Score
24. score = 0
25.
26. #Repeat 10 times
27. for q in range(1,11):
28.   print("Question " + str(q) + ":")
29.
30.   #Generate random question
31.   operand1 = random.randint(0,12)
32.   operand2 = random.randint(0,12)
33.   operator = random.choice(["+","-","x"])
34.   question = str(operand1) + operator + str(operand2) + "?"
35.
36.   #Calculate correct answer
```

```
37.    correctAnswer = 0
38.    if operator=="+":
39.      correctAnswer = operand1 + operand2
40.    elif operator=="-":
41.      correctAnswer = operand1 - operand2
42.    elif operator=="x":
43.      correctAnswer = operand1 * operand2
44.
45.    #Retrieve user answer
46.    userAnswer = inputNumber(question)
47.
48.    #Check if user is correct
49.    if userAnswer==correctAnswer:
50.      score += 10
51.      print("Good answer!")
52.    else:
53.      score -= 5
54.      print("Incorrect! The correct answer was " + str(correct
      Answer))
55.
56. #Display total score /100
57. print("+-x End of Quiz x-+")
58. print("Total Score: " + str(score) + "%")
```

34. Higher or Lower Game

For this challenge you will design and write a program to play against the computer. The computer will display a random number between 1 and 1000. It will then ask the end-user whether they believe the next number will be higher or lower. The program will then generate the next number. If the user guessed right (e.g. the next number is higher or lower than the previous one) then the user scores one point. The game stops when the user guess is wrong.

Web Address
http://www.101computing.net/higher-or-lower/

Python Code

```
1.  #Higher or Lower Game - www.101computing.net/higher-or-
    lower/
2.  from random import randint
3.
4.  #Initialise the game
5.  number=randint(1,1000)
6.  score=0
7.
8.  while True:
9.      print("Current Number: " + str(number))
10.
11.     #Collect user guess
12.     userGuess = input("Will the next number be higher (type +)
        or lower (type -)?")
13.
14.     #Generate next number
15.     nextNumber=randint (1,1000)
16.     print("Next number is: " + str(nextNumber))
17.
18.     #Check if the user is correct
19.     if userGuess=="+" and nextNumber >= number:
20.         score+=1
21.         number=nextNumber
22.     elif userGuess=="-" and nextNumber <= number:
23.         score+=1
24.         number=nextNumber
25.     else:
26.         print "Game over"
27.         break
28.
29.     #Display score so far
30.     print ("Your score is: " + str(score))
```

35. Guess the Number (Player vs. Computer)

For this challenge, we will get the computer to randomly pick a number between 0 and 100. Let the user try to guess what this number is. The computer will inform the user if they guessed the number or whether their guess is too high or too low. The program will count and display the number of guesses used to guess the correct number.

http://www.101computing.net/my-first-python-game-guess-the-number/

Python Code

```
1.  #Guess the number - www.101computing.net
2.  import random
3.
4.  #Generate a Random Number between 0 and 100 and store it as
    'numberToguess'
5.  numberToGuess=random.randint(0,100)
6.
7.  userGuess = -1
8.  numberOfGuesses = 0
9.
10. while userGuess!=numberToGuess:
11.     #Get the user to enter a number using the 'input' functi
    on and convert in to an Integer suing the 'int' function
12.     userGuess=int(input("Guess the number (between 1 and 100
    )"))
13.     numberOfGuesses += 1
14.
15.     #Compare this number, userGuess, with the numberToGuess.
    Display the right message if the userGuess is greater than,
    lower than or equal to the numberToGuess
16.     if userGuess>numberToGuess:
17.         print("Too high!")
18.     elif userGuess<numberToGuess:
19.         print("Too low!")
20.     elif userGuess==numberToGuess:
21.         print("Good guess, the number to guess was " + str(n
    umberToGuess) + " indeed.")
22.         print("You guessed it in " + str(numberOfGuesses) +
    " attempts.")
23.         #Eng of game - exit the while loop
24.         break
```

36. Guess the Number (Computer vs. Player)

Before attempting this challenge, make sure you have completed the previous challenge first, Guess the number, player vs. computer.

In this version the player will be asked to enter a number between 1 and 100. The computer will then use a binary search algorithm to try to guess the correct number keeping the number of guesses to a minimum.

The binary search is a very effective algorithm to search through a large list that is already sorted, in our case the list of numbers from 1 to 100. It is based on the following flowchart:

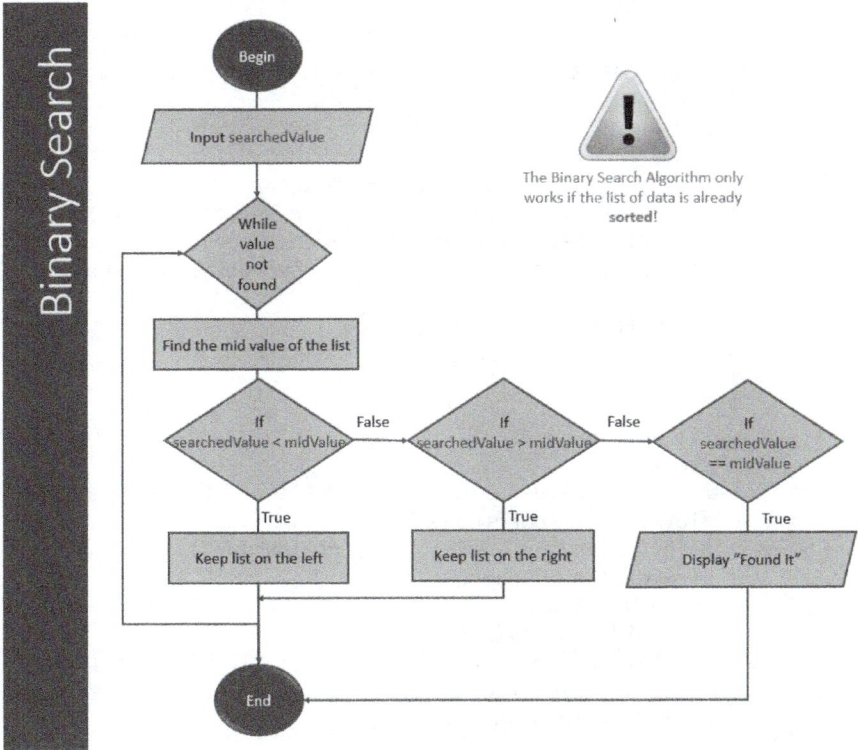

Web Address

http:// www.101computing.net/guess-the-number-binary-search/

Python Code

```
1.  #Guess the Number vs Computer - www.101computing.net/guess-
    the-number-binary-search/
```

80

```
2.
3.  #A function to input a number
4.  def inputNumber(message):
5.    while True:
6.      try:
7.        userInput = int(input(message))
8.      except ValueError:
9.        print("Not an integer! Try again.")
10.       continue
11.     else:
12.       return userInput
13.       break
14.
15. #MAIN PROGRAM STARTS HERE:
16. lower = 0
17. upper = 101
18.
19. #Retrieve and validate number to guess
20. number = inputNumber("Type a number between 1 and 100?")
21. while not (number>=lower and number<upper):
22.   number = inputNumber("Type a number between 1 and 100?")
23.
24. found = False
25. steps = 0
26.
27. #Implement Binary Search
28. while not found:
29.   steps+=1
30.   #Calculate mid-value
31.   midValue = (lower+upper)//2
32.   print("Computer Guess: " + str(midValue))
33.   if midValue == number:
34.     found = True
35.   elif midValue>number:
36.     print("Lower...")
37.     upper = midValue
38.   elif midValue<number:
39.     print("Higher...")
40.     lower = midValue
41.
42. print("Number: " + str(midValue))
43. print("Found in " + str(steps) + " steps.")
```

37. Limit 33 Game

"Limit 33" is a simple game of adding a series of random numbers to a running total. The player's aim is to reach a total as close as possible to 33 without taking this total over 33.

Rules of the Game

1. A player starts with a total of zero.
2. On each turn a random number between 1 and 10 is generated and added to the player's total.
3. If the player's total exceeds 33, the player has lost and the game ends: Game Over.
4. At the end of each turn the player is asked whether they want to complete another turn or quit.
5. If they quit, the player is given a score as follows:
   - Zero point if their total is below 24 or above 33.
   - $10 \times (total - 23)$ points if their total is between 24 and 33.
   - For instance with a total of 29, the player would score $10 \times (29-23) = 60$ points. The maximum score they can reach is $10 \times (33-23) = 100$ when they reach a total of 33!

Web Address

http://www.101computing.net/limit-33/

Python Code

```
1.  # Limit 33 - www.101computing.net/limit-33/
2.  import random
3.
4.  score = 0
5.  total = 0
6.
7.  carryOn = input("Are you ready?")
8.
```

```
9.  while (total<33 and carryOn=="yes"):
10.    randomNumber = random.randint(1,10)
11.    total = total + randomNumber
12.    print ("Your total is:" + str(total))
13.    carryOn = input("Do you want to carry on?")
14.
15. if total<24:
16.    print "Game Over!"
17.    print "Zero point scored"
18. elif total>33:
19.    print "Game Over!"
20.    print "You have exceeded 33!"
21.    print "Zero point scored"
22. else:
23.    print "Game Over!"
24.    score = 10 * (total -23)
25.    print "Your score: " + str(score)
```

38. Roulette

In this betting game of Roulette a player starts the game with 10 chips.

For each game the player should be asked how many chips they want to bet. They should not be allowed to bet more chips than they actually own.

Then the user should be asked which number they want to bet on (between 0 and 10).

The user should be asked which colour they want to bet on:
- Green (Number 0),
- Red (for odd numbers),
- Black (for even numbers).

The computer program should then "spin the wheel" by generating a random number between 0 and 10.

- If the number generated matches the user's number then the user should be given 10 times their initial bet.
- If the number generated matches the user's colour (green for 0, red for an odd number, black for an even number) then the user should be given twice their initial bet.
- If none of the above two conditions are met, the user loses their bet.

At the end of each bet, the program should display the user's total number of chips.

The player should be able to carry on playing for as long as they want unless they have lost all their chips. In this case the game should end.

Web Address

http://www.101computing.net/roulette-betting-game/

Python Code

```
1.  #Roulette Challenge - 101computing.net/roulette
2.  from random import randint
3.
4.  numberOfChips = 10
5.
6.  while (numberOfChips>0):
7.    print("\nYou currently have " + str(numberOfChips) + " chi
      ps.")
8.
9.    #Place a bet
10.   betValue = int(input("You currently have " + str(numberOfC
      hips) + " chips.\nHow many chips would you want to bet?"))
11.   while (betValue > numberOfChips):
12.     print("This bet is too high. You only have " + str(numbe
        rOfChips) + " chips left.")
13.     betValue=int(input("Maximum bet: " + str(numberOfChips)
        + " How many chips would you want to bet?"))
14.
15.   betNumber = int(input("What number do you want to be on?")
      )
16.   while (betNumber<0 or betNumber>10):
```

```
17.      print("You can only bet on a number between 0 and 10")

18.      betNumber = int(input("What number do you want to be on?
         "))
19.
20.  betColor = input("What color woul dyou want to bet on: R f
     or Red, B for Black or G for Green?").upper()
21.  while (betColor != "B" and betColor != "R" and betColor !=
     "G"):
22.      print("This bet is too high. You only have " + str(numbe
     rOfChips) + " chips left.")
23.      betColor = input("What color woul dyou want to bet on: R
     for Red, B for Black or G for Green?").upper()
24.
25.  print("You are placing a bet of " + str(betValue)  + " chi
     ps on number: " + str(betNumber) + " and color " + betColor
     + ".")
26.
27.  #let's spin the wheel!
28.  print("Let's spin the wheel")
29.  randomNumber=randint(0,10)
30.  if randomNumber==0:
31.    color="G"
32.    colorDescription="Green"
33.  else:
34.    if randomNumber%2==0: #Even numbers are black
35.      color="B"
36.      colorDescription="Black"
37.    else: #Odd numbers are red
38.      color="R"
39.      colorDescription="Red"
40.
41.  print("The white ball stopped on " + str(randomNumber) + "
     , colour " + colorDescription)
42.
43.  #Check the if the bet was right and calculate winnings
44.  numberOfChips = numberOfChips - betValue
45.  win=False
46.  if randomNumber==betNumber:
47.    numberOfChips=numberOfChips + 10*betValue
48.    print("Lucky you! You did bet on the right number!")
49.    win=True
50.  if (color==betColor):
51.    numberOfChips=numberOfChips + 2*betValue
52.    print("Lucky you! You did bet on the right colour!")
53.    win=True
54.  if win==False:
55.    print("Unlucky you did not win anything win with this be
     t!")
```

85

```
56.
57. print("\n\nSorry you have no more chips! Game over")
```

39. Ten-Pin Bowling Scoreboard

The aim of this challenge is to create a scoreboard for a game of ten-pin bowling. It will be used to automatically calculate the total score of a player as they progress through the ten rounds of the game.

The scoring system in a game of ten-pin bowling is fairly complex to understand. Check the link provided below to fully understand the scoring system before attempting to complete this challenge.

Ten-pin Bowling – Scoring System

https://en.wikipedia.org/wiki/Ten-pin_bowling#Scoring

Web Address

http://www.101computing.net/bowling-scoreboard/

Python Code
```
1.  #Bowling Scoreboard - www.101computing.net/bowling-
    scoreboard/
2.
3.  #A function to ask the user to enter a valid score
4.  def inputScore(message):
5.    validScore=False
6.    while validScore==False:
7.      #Accept whole numbers only
8.      try:
9.        score = int(input(message))
10.     except ValueError:
11.       print("You must enter an integer.\n")
12.     else:
13.       #A valid score is between 0 and 10
14.       if score<0 or score>10:
15.         print("You must enter a score between 0 and 10.")
16.       else:
17.         validScore=True
```

```
18.    return score
19.
20. scores=[]
21.
22. #There are 10 rounds in a game:
23. for round in range(0,10):
24.    #Up to two throws per round:
25.    print("\n######### Round : " + str(round+1) + " ##########
    ##")
26.    firstThrow=inputScore("Throw 1: ")
27.
28.    if firstThrow<10:
29.      secondThrow=inputScore("Throw 2: ")
30.      if firstThrow + secondThrow == 10:
31.        print(" */*/*/*/* SPARE  */*/*/*/*")
32.    else:
33.      print(" *X*X*X*X* STRIKE  *X*X*X*X*")
34.      secondThrow=0 #No second throw as you did a strike
35.
36.    scores.append([firstThrow, secondThrow, firstThrow + secon
    dThrow])
37.
38.    #Now Let's check if the previous round was a Strike.
39.    #If so we will add the score of both throws to the score o
    f the previous round
40.    #Note that we can only check the previous round if we are
    on round 2 or above.
41.
42.    if round>=1:
43.      if scores[round-
    1][0]==10: #Previous Round was a strike
44.        scores[round-1][2] += (firstThrow + secondThrow)
45.
46.        #In case of a double strike we can now check if round[
    -2] was a strike too!
47.        #If that's the case then we add the score of the first
    Throw to the round[-2] score
48.        #Note that we can only check round[-
    2] if we are on the third round or above
49.        if round>=2:
50.          if scores[round-2][0]==10: #Round[-2] was a strike
51.            scores[round-2][2] += firstThrow
52.
53.      #If the previous round was not a strike it might have be
    en a spare
54.      elif (scores[round-1][0] + scores[round-1][1])==10:
55.        scores[round-1][2] += firstThrow
56.
57.    print(scores)
```

87

```
58.
59.    #Calculate the cumulative score...
60.    totalScore = 0
61.    for roundScores in scores:
62.        totalScore += roundScores[2]
63.    print("Total Score: " + str(totalScore))
64.
65. #If the user finished with a strike (round 10) they get two
    extra throws:
66. if scores[9][0]==10:
67.        firstThrow=inputScore("Extra Throw 1: ")
68.        secondThrow=inputScore("Extra Throw 2: ")
69.        scores[9][2] = 10 + firstThrow + secondThrow
70.        #If round 9 was aso a strike, the score of the first ext
    ra throw is also counting for round 9.
71.        if scores[8,0]==10:
72.            scores[8][2] += firstThrow
73. elif scores[9][2]==10:
74. #If the user finished with a spare (round 10) they get one e
    xtra throw:
75.        firstThrow=inputScore("Extra Throw: ")
76.        scores[9][2] = 10 + firstThrow
77.
78. #Calculate the cumulative score...
79. totalScore = 0
80. for roundScores in scores:
81.    totalScore += roundScores[2]
82. print("Total Score: " + str(totalScore))
83.
84. print("Game Over!")
```

40. Mastermind Challenge

For this challenge we are going to create a game of mastermind where the end-user plays against the computer. The end-user's role is to guess the secret combination of four colours randomly selected by the computer.

If you are not too sure about the rules of this game, you should first check this page: https://en.wikipedia.org/wiki/Mastermind_(board_game)

http://www.101computing.net/mastermind-challenge/

Python Code

```
1.  #Mastermind Challenge - www.101computing.net/mastermind-
    challenge
2.  import random
3.
4.  #Let the computer choose a combination of 4 colours
5.  colors = ["Black", "White", "Red", "Yellow", "Blue", "Green"
    ]
6.  computerColor1 = random.choice(colors)
7.  computerColor2 = random.choice(colors)
8.  computerColor3 = random.choice(colors)
9.  computerColor4 = random.choice(colors)
10.
11. #For testing purposes only display the 4 colours!
12. #print(computerColor1 + " " + computerColor2 + " " + compute
    rColor3 + " " + computerColor4)
13.
14. #Let's give the user up to 10 guesses
15. for i in range(1,11):
16.    #User input
17.    userColor1=input("Color 1?")
18.    userColor2=input("Color 2?")
19.    userColor3=input("Color 3?")
20.    userColor4=input("Color 4?")
21.
22.    #Let's compare user's guess with the actual combination
23.    pegsInRightPosition=0
24.    pegsMisplaced=0
25.    if userColor1==computerColor1:
26.       pegsInRightPosition+=1
27.    else:
28.       if userColor1==computerColor2 or userColor1==computerCol
    or3 or userColor1==computerColor4:
29.          pegsMisplaced+=1
30.
31.    if userColor2==computerColor2:
32.       pegsInRightPosition+=1
33.    else:
34.       if userColor2==computerColor1 or userColor2==computerCol
    or3 or userColor2==computerColor4:
35.          pegsMisplaced+=1
36.
37.    if userColor3==computerColor3:
38.       pegsInRightPosition+=1
```

89

```
39.    else:
40.       if userColor3==computerColor2 or userColor3==computerCol
   or1 or userColor3==computerColor4:
41.          pegsMisplaced+=1
42.
43.    if userColor4==computerColor4:
44.       pegsInRightPosition+=1
45.    else:
46.       if userColor4==computerColor2 or userColor4==computerCol
   or3 or userColor4==computerColor2:
47.          pegsMisplaced+=1
48.
49.    #Output results to the user
50.    print("Correct Pegs: " + str(pegsInRightPosition))
51.    print("Misplaced Pegs: " + str(pegsMisplaced))
52.
53.    #Did the user guess all four colours?
54.    if pegsInRightPosition==4:
55.       break
56.
57. #Final output
58. if pegsInRightPosition==4:
59.    print("*********** You Win ************")
60. else:
61.    print("*********** Game Over ************")
```

Chapter #4: Subroutines

As we are now working on more complex programs, our code listings become fairly long. One approach to organise our code more effectively is to use **subroutines** so that functional sections of code can be grouped into subroutines. This makes it easy to read, understand and troubleshoot the code. Subroutines, such as **functions** and **procedures**, are also very useful as they allow you to call them whenever you need them. This reduces the need to duplicate lines of code within your program when the same functionality is required at different stages of your program.

Finally, you may write some subroutines that could be reused within other programs. This is a lot easier to do when the code is organised into subroutines. To facilitate code reusability of your subroutines you may also want to create your own **library**. A library is a collection of subroutines with a common theme. For instance in challenge 44 you will create your own library of conversions functions.

Another aspect of functions is that they enable us to implement a forth programming construct called **recursion**. (Remember so far we have only used three programming constructs: sequencing, selection and iteration). To investigate how a recursive algorithm works, you can jump to challenge 96.

In this chapter we will investigate:

- Functions and Procedures,
- Passing Parameters,
- Creating a Python Library,
- Recursive Algorithms.

FUNCTION()

41. Area Calculator

For this challenge we are going to use a Python script to calculate the area in square meters of a mansion. To do so we will write a computer program that will add up all the areas of each room. We will create two functions to retrieve the area of a rectangle (area = width * length) and the area of a right-angled triangle (area = width * length / 2).

Below is the picture of the mansion that we will use for our program.

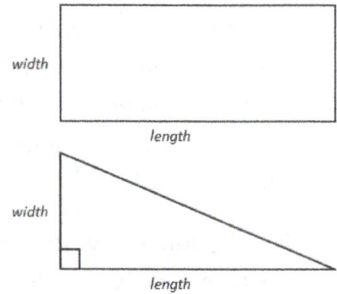

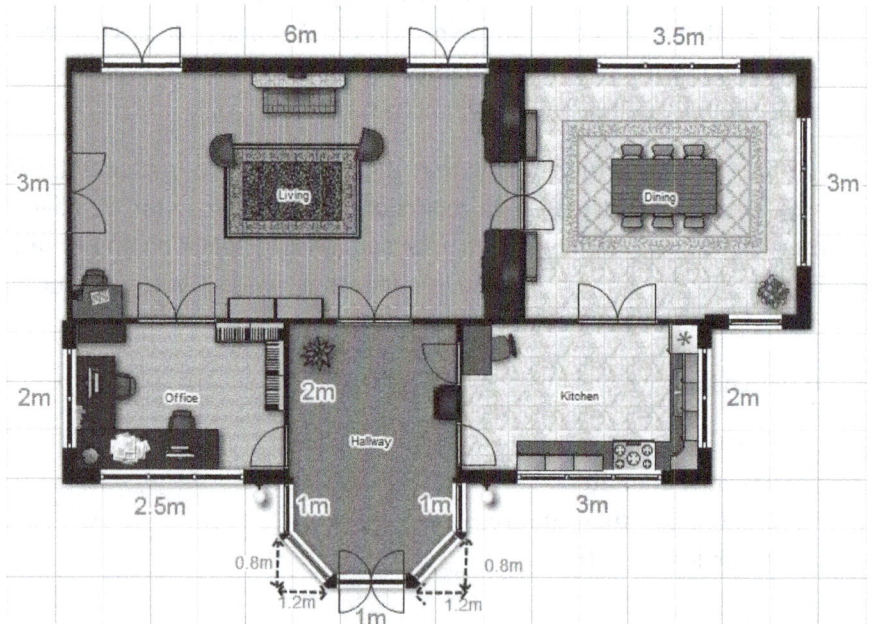

Web Address

http://www.101computing.net/area-calculator/

```
1.  #Area Calculator  -  www.101computing.net/area-calculator
2.
3.  def getRectangleArea(width, length):
4.    area = width * length
5.    return area
6.
7.  def getTriangleArea(width, length):
8.    area = width * length / 2
9.    return area
10.
11. #Calculate area of each room
12. living = getRectangleArea(3,6)
13. dining = getRectangleArea(3.5,3)
14. office = getRectangleArea(2.5,2)
15. kitchen = getRectangleArea(3,2)
16. hallway = getRectangleArea(3.4,3.8) -
      2 * getTriangleArea(1.2,0.8)
17.
18. #Find out total area by adding area of each room
19. totalArea = living + dining + office + kitchen + hallway
20.
21. #Output total area
22. print("This flat has an area of " + str(totalArea) + " squar
      e meters")
```

42. Volume Calculator

By completing this challenge we are going to learn how to define our own functions in Python.
We will also assign parameters to our functions.

We will create four functions as follows:
- *getVolumeOfCube(width)*
- *getVolumeOfCylinder(radius, height)*
- *getVolumeOfCuboid(width, length, height)*
- *getVolumeOfCone(radius, height)*

We will then use our formulas to calculate the volume of each of these four bottles:

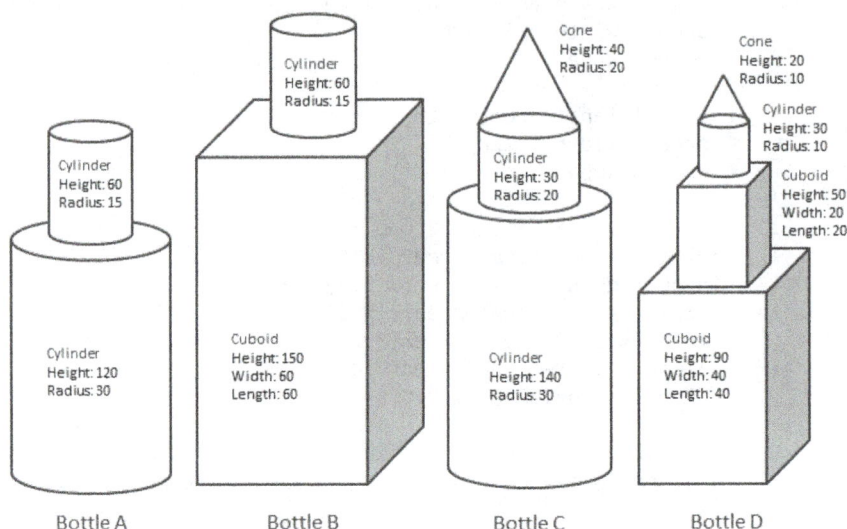

Cylinder
Height: 60
Radius: 15

Cylinder
Height: 60
Radius: 15

Cone
Height: 40
Radius: 20

Cone
Height: 20
Radius: 10

Cylinder
Height: 30
Radius: 20

Cylinder
Height: 30
Radius: 10

Cuboid
Height: 50
Width: 20
Length: 20

Cylinder
Height: 120
Radius: 30

Cuboid
Height: 150
Width: 60
Length: 60

Cylinder
Height: 140
Radius: 30

Cuboid
Height: 90
Width: 40
Length: 40

Bottle A   Bottle B   Bottle C   Bottle D

Web Address
http://www.101computing.net/volume-calculator/

Python Code

```
1.  #Volume Calculator - www.101computing.net/volume-
    calculator/
2.
3.  def getVolumeOfCube(width):
4.      volume = width * width * width
5.      #This calculates the volume in cubic millimeters. Divide
    it by 1000 to get this volume in mL
6.      volume=volume/1000
7.      return volume
8.
9.  def getVolumeOfCuboid(length,width,height):
10.     volume = length * width * height
11.     #This calculates the volume in cubic millimeters. Divide
    it by 1000 to get this volume in mL
12.     volume=volume/1000
```

```
13.        return volume
14.
15. def getVolumeOfCylinder(radius, height):
16.        volume = (3.14 * (radius ** 2)) * height
17.        #This calculates the volume in cubic millimeters. Divide
   it by 1000 to get this volume in mL
18.        volume=volume/1000
19.        return volume
20.
21. def getVolumeOfCone(radius, height):
22.        volume = (3.14 * (radius ** 2)) * height / 3
23.        #This calculates the volume in cubic millimeters. Divide
   it by 1000 to get this volume in mL
24.        volume=volume/1000
25.        return volume
26.
27. #Main Program Starts Here
28. #Bottle A
29. volume1 = getVolumeOfCylinder(30,120)
30. volume2 = getVolumeOfCylinder(15,60)
31. bottleA = volume1 + volume2
32. print("The volume bottle A is: " + str(bottleA) + " mL.")
33.
34. #Bottle B
35. volume1 = getVolumeOfCuboid(60,60,150)
36. volume2 = getVolumeOfCylinder(15,60)
37. bottleB = volume1 + volume2
38. print("The volume bottle B is: " + str(bottleB) + " mL.")
39.
40. #Bottle C
41. volume1 = getVolumeOfCylinder(30,140)
42. volume2 = getVolumeOfCylinder(20,30)
43. volume3 = getVolumeOfCone(20,40)
44. bottleC = volume1 + volume2 + volume3
45. print("The volume bottle C is: " + str(bottleC) + " mL.")
46.
47. #Bottle D
48. volume1 = getVolumeOfCuboid(40,40,90)
49. volume2 = getVolumeOfCuboid(20,20,50)
50. volume3 = getVolumeOfCylinder(10,30)
51. volume4 = getVolumeOfCone(10,20)
52. bottleD = volume1 + volume2 + volume3 + volume4
53. print("The volume bottle D is: " + str(bottleD) + " mL.")
```

43. Find the Monster

The aim of this text-based game is to open as many doors as possible without meeting the monster. At the start of the game, the user is facing three doors. They have to decide which door they will use to escape the room they are in. If they do not meet a monster the game carries on with another three doors. Each time the user manages to escape a room without meeting the monster they score one point. The game ends when the user meets the monster.

Web Address

http://www.101computing.net/find-the-monster/

Python Code

```
1.  #Find the monster! www.101computing.net/find-the-monster
2.  import random
3.
4.  #A function to draw 3 doors on screen
5.  def doors():
6.      print '''''
7.        _____1_____      _____2____      ____3_____
8.      |  __   __  |    |  __   __  |    |  __   __  |
9.      | | || |  | |    | | || |  | |    | | || |  | |
10.     | |_||_|  | |    | |_||_|  | |    | |_||_|  | |
11.     | |__||__| |     | |__||__| |     | |__||__| |
12.     |  __   __()|    |  __   __()|    |  __   __()|
13.     | | || |  | |    | | || |  | |    | | || |  | |
14.     | | || |  | |    | | || |  | |    | | || |  | |
15.     | | || |  | |    | | || |  | |    | | || |  | |
16.     | | || |  | |    | | || |  | |    | | || |  | |
17.     | |__||__| |     | |__||__| |     | |__||__| |
18.     |_____|    |_____|    |_____|' ' '
19.
20. #A function to draw the ugly monster on screen
21. def monster():
22.     print '''''
23.          .-""-"_-""-.
24.         | .--.-.--. |
25.         |`  >       `|
26.         |  <        |
27.         (__..---..__)
```

```
28.        (`|\o_/ \_o/|`)
29.        \(     >     )/
30.      [>=|    vvv    |=<]
31.        \__\   /__/
32.             '_'
33. '''
34. print ("~~~~~~~~~~~~~~~~~~~~~~~~~~~~")
35. print ("~                        ~")
36. print ("~ Avoid the monster! ~")
37. print ("~                        ~")
38. print ("~~~~~~~~~~~~~~~~~~~~~~~~~~~~")
39.
40. #Initialise the game
41. score = 0
42. carryOn = True
43.
44. #Start playing
45. while carryOn:
46.    #Monster is randomly hiding behing one of the three doors

47.    monsterDoor = random.randint(1, 3)
48.    print ("Three doors ahead...")
49.    doors()
50.    print ("Is the Monster behind door...")
51.    userDoor = int(input("1,2, or 3?"))
52.    if userDoor ==  monsterDoor:
53.       print (" ARGHHH! MONSTER")
54.       monster()
55.       #End the while the loop
56.       carryOn=False
57.    else:
58.       print("Phew! No Monster!")
59.       #Increment Score
60.       score += 1
61.       print("You enter the next room.")
62.
63. #Game Over - Display Final Score
64. print("Game Over - Final Score: " + str(score))
```

44. My Conversion Library

In this challenge we will create our own library of
python functions used to perform various unit
conversions. A library is a collection of functions and
procedures. A library can then be reused in other programs using the
import instruction. We have already used existing libraries in some of the
previous challenges such as the random library or the maths library.

We are now going to create our own library focusing on conversion
formulas. It will be useful when we need to convert for example distances
from one unit to another (e.g. miles to km, cm to inches). We will focus on
the following conversions:

Distance Conversions:

km to miles	1 mile = 1.609 km
cm to inches	1 inch = 2.54 cm

Weight Conversions:

Kilogram to pounds and ounces	1 kg = 2.2046226218 pounds
	1 pound = 16 ounces
Kilogram to stones and pounds	1 stone = 6.35029318 kg
	1 stone = 14 pounds

Temperature Conversions:

Celsius Degrees (^{o}C)	^{o}C = (^{o}F − 32) x 5 / 9
Fahrenheit Degrees (^{o}F)	^{o}F = (^{o}C x 9 / 5) + 32

Time Conversions:

seconds	HH:MM:SS
	1 Minute = 60 seconds
	1 Hour = 60 minutes
	1 Hour = 3600 seconds

http://www.101computing.net/my-conversion-library/

Python Code: Conversion Library – conversion.py

```
1.  #Conversion Library - www.101computing.net/my-conversion-
    library/
2.
3.  #Distance Conversion
4.  def milesToKm(miles):
5.      km = miles * 1.609
6.      return km
7.
8.  def kmToMiles(km):
9.      miles = km / 1.609
10.     return miles
11.
12. def cmToInches(cm):
13.     inches = cm / 2.54
14.     return inches
15.
16. def inchesToCm(inches):
17.     cm = inches * 2.54
18.     return cm
19.
20. #Weight Conversion
21. def kgToLboz(kg):
22.     tmp = kg *  2.20462
23.     lb = int(tmp)
24.     oz = (tmp-lb) * 16
25.     return [lb,oz]
26.
27. def lbozToKg(lb,oz):
28.     kg = (lb + oz / 16) / 2.20462;
29.     return kg
30.
31. def kgTostlb(kg):
32.     tmp = kg / 6.3503
33.     st = int(tmp)
34.     lb = (tmp-st) * 14
35.     return [st,lb]
36.
37. def stlbToKg(st,lb):
38.     kg = (st + lb / 14) * 6.3503;
39.     return kg
40.
41. #Temperature Conversion
42. def celsiusToFahrenheit(celsius):
```

```
43.     fahrenheit = (celsius * 9 / 5) + 32
44.     return fahrenheit
45.
46. def fahrenheitToCelsius(fahrenheit):
47.     celsius = (fahrenheit - 32) * 5 / 9
48.     return celsius
49.
50. #Time Conversion
51. def formatTime(seconds):
52.     hours = seconds // 3600
53.     remainer = seconds % 3600
54.     minutes = remainer // 60
55.     seconds = remainer % 60
56.     if hours<10:
57.         hours = "0" + str(hours)
58.     else:
59.         hours = str(hours)
60.     if minutes<10:
61.         minutes = "0" + str(minutes)
62.     else:
63.         minutes = str(minutes)
64.     if seconds<10:
65.         seconds = "0" + str(seconds)
66.     else:
67.         seconds = str(seconds)
68.
69.     time = hours + ":" + minutes + ":" + seconds
70.     return time
```

Python Code: Using the library – main.py

```
1.  #Conversion Challenge - www.101computing.net/my-conversion-
    library/
2.  from conversion import *
3.
4.  print("######################")
5.  print("#   Conversion Tools   #")
6.  print("######################")
7.  print("")
8.  print(" 1 - Miles to km")
9.  print(" 2 - km to Miles")
10. print(" 3 - Inches to cm")
11. print(" 4 - cm to inches")
12. print(" 5 - Kg to Stones and Pounds")
13. print(" 6 - Kg to Pounds and Ounces")
14. print(" 7 - Celsius to Fahrenheit")
15. print(" 8 - Fahrenheit to Celsius")
16. print(" 9 - Seconds to HH:MM:SS")
17. print("")
```

```
18. option = input("1 to 9?")
19.
20. if option == "1":
21.     distance = float(input("Distance in miles?"))
22.     distanceInKm = milesToKm(distance)
23.     print(str(distance) + " miles = " + str(distanceInKm) + "
    km")
24. elif option == "2":
25.     distance = float(input("Distance in km?"))
26.     distanceInMiles = kmToMiles(distance)
27.     print(str(distance) + " km = " + str(distanceInMiles) + "
    miles")
28. elif option == "3":
29.     distance = float(input("Distance in inches?"))
30.     distanceInCm = inchesToCm(distance)
31.     print(str(distance) + " inches = " + str(distanceInCm) + "
    cm")
32. elif option == "4":
33.     distance = float(input("Distance in cm?"))
34.     distanceInInches = cmToInches(distance)
35.     print(str(distance) + " cm = " + str(distanceInInches) + "
    inches")
36. elif option == "5":
37.     kg = float(input("Weight in kg?"))
38.     stlb = kgTostlb(kg)
39.     print(str(kg) + "kg = " + str(stlb[0]) + " stones and "+ s
    tr(stlb[1]) + " pounds")
40. elif option == "6":
41.     kg = float(input("Weight in kg?"))
42.     lboz = kgToLboz(kg)
43.     print(str(kg) + "kg = " + str(lboz[0]) + " pounds and "+ s
    tr(lboz[1]) + " ounces")
44. elif option == "7":
45.     celsius = float(input("Temperature in Celsius?"))
46.     fahrenheit = celsiusToFahrenheit(celsius)
47.     print(str(celsius) + " Celsius deg. = " + str(fahrenheit)
    + " Fahrenheit deg.")
48. elif option == "8":
49.     fahrenheit = float(input("Temperature in Fahrenheit?"))
50.     celsius = fahrenheitToCelsius(fahrenheit)
51.     print(str(fahrenheit) + " Fahrenheit deg. = " + str(celsiu
    s) + " Celsius deg.")
52. elif option == "9":
53.     seconds = int(input("Number of seconds?"))
54.     print(formatTime(seconds))
55. else:
56.     print("Invalid menu option.")
```

45. RGB - Hex Converter

Did you know that every colour on the screen can be represented using an RGB code (Red, Green, Blue). This code consists of three numbers between 0 and 255, indicating how much red, green and blue are used to recreate the colour. For instance the RGB code for:

- Red is (255,0,0)
- Green is (0,255,0)
- Blue is (0,0,255)
- Yellow is (255,255,0)
- Orange is (255,165,0)

Graphic designers and software programmers sometimes prefer to use another notation based on hexadecimal RGB code where each of the three decimal values are converted into a two-digit hexadecimal code, resulting in a 6-digit (3x2) hexadecimal code. For instance:

- Red is #FF000
- Green is #00FF00
- Blue is #0000FF
- Yellow is #FFFF00
- Orange is #FFA500

The aim of this challenge is to write a program to perform decimal RGB to hexadecimal colour code conversions and vice-versa.

Web Address

http://www.101computing.net/RGB-converter/

Colour Picker: Pick a colour and find its RGB colour code

http://www.colorpicker.com

Python Code

```
1.  #RGB to Hex Colour Converter - www.101computing.net/RGB-
    converter/
```

```
2.
3.  #Hexadecimal to Decimal (RGB) conversion
4.  def hexToRgb(hex):
5.      hex = hex.lstrip('#')
6.      hexchars = "0123456789ABCDEF"
7.      red = hexchars.index(hex[0])*16 + hexchars.index(hex[1])
8.      green = hexchars.index(hex[2])*16 + hexchars.index(hex[3])
9.      blue = hexchars.index(hex[4])*16 + hexchars.index(hex[5])

10.     return [red,green,blue]
11.
12. #Decimal (RGB) To Hexadecimal conversion
13. def rgbToHex(red,green,blue):
14.     hexchars = "0123456789ABCDEF"
15.     hexRed = hexchars[red // 16] + hexchars[red % 16]
16.     hexGreen = hexchars[green // 16] + hexchars[green % 16]

17.     hexBlue = hexchars[blue // 16] + hexchars[blue % 16]
18.     return "#" +  hexRed + hexGreen + hexBlue
19.
20. #Main Program Starts Here
21. print("RGB Converter Options:")
22. print(" 1 - Hexadecimal to Decimal (RGB) conversion")
23. print(" 2 - Decimal (RGB) To Hexadecimal conversion")
24. option = input("Choose an option, 1 or 2:")
25.
26. if option=="1":
27.     #Hexadecimal to Decimal (RGB) conversion
28.     colour = input("Enter a colour code in hexadecial e.g. #F3
        AB04:")
29.     print("RGB:" + str(hexToRgb(colour)))
30. elif option=="2":
31.     #Decimal (RGB) To Hexadecimal conversion
32.     red = int(input("Input red value (0 to 255):"))
33.     green = int(input("Input green value (0 to 255):"))
34.     blue = int(input("Input blue value (0 to 255):"))
35.     print("Colour Code: " + rgbToHex(red,green,blue))
36. else:
37.     print("Invalid option!")
```

Chapter #5: Data Structures

In most, if not all our challenges so far, we have used variables to store values within our code. Each variable was used to store a single value: an integer, a float, a Boolean or a string.

In Python, it is also possible to store a collection of values within a variable. Such a variable is called a **list**.

An alternative data structure that can also be used in Python is a **dictionary**. By completing the next few challenges you will gain a good understanding of the similarities and differences between lists and dictionaries.

The next few challenges focus on the use of lists and dictionaries within a Python program and will cover:

- Using Lists in Python,
- Using a List of Lists,
- Using Dictionaries.

46. Quote of the Day

In Python, a list is used to save a collection of values. For instance, to save all the different days of the week, we could declare a variable called "daysOfTheWeek" and assign a list as follows (Notice the use of square brackets):

```
daysOfTheWeek = ["Monday", "Tuesday", "Wednesday",
"Thursday", "Friday", "Saturday", "Sunday"]
```

In this challenge we decided to create three lists to store:
1. A collection of inspirational quotes,
2. A collection of French words,
3. A list of arithmetic operators, +,-,x,/

We will then randomly pick a value from each list to display so that each time we run our program it will display:
1. The quote of the day,
2. The French word of the day,
3. A random maths based challenge using one of the four arithmetic operators.

Web Address

http://www.101computing.net/quote-of-the-day/

Python Code

```
1.  # Quote of the day - www.101computing.net/quote-of-the-day
2.  import random
3.
4.  #Initialise an empty list that will be stored our bank of qu
    otes
5.  quotes = []
6.
7.  #Append a few quotes to our list
8.  quotes.append("The harder I work, the luckier I get.")
9.  quotes.append("A person who never made a mistake never tried
    anything new.")
10. quotes.append("Nothing will work unless you do.")
```

```python
11. quotes.append("The best preparation for good work tomorrow i
    s to do good work today.")
12. quotes.append("Choose a job you love, and you will never hav
    e to work a day in your life.")
13.
14. #Randomly pick a quote from our bank of quotes
15. dailyQuote = random.choice(quotes)
16.
17. print("")
18. print("##########################")
19. print("#     Quote of the Day    #")
20. print("##########################")
21. print("")
22. print(dailyQuote)
23. print("")
24. #French Word of the Day:
25. words = ["Bonjour","Au Revoir","Merci","Bleu","Blanc","Rouge
    "]
26. dailyWord = random.choice(words)
27. print("##########################")
28. print("#  French Word of the Day  #")
29. print("##########################")
30. print("")
31. print(dailyWord)
32. print("")
33. #Maths Challenge of the Day:
34. operand1 = random.randint(0,100)
35. operand2 = random.randint(0,100)
36. operator = random.choice(["+","-","x","/"])
37. dailyChallenge = str(operand1) + operator + str(operand2) +
    "?"
38. print("##########################")
39. print("#    Daly Maths Challenge   #")
40. print("##########################")
41. print("")
42. print(dailyChallenge)
```

47. The Gruffalo

This challenge is inspired from Julia Donaldson and
Alex Sheffler's children book: "The Gruffalo". In this
story a little mouse describes a ferocious
animal/monster called a "Gruffalo" to scare other dangerous animals (fox,

snake, owl) she encounters while taking a walk in the forest. This little mouse being very imaginative, she uses plenty of frightening adjectives to describe this fictional animal.

In this challenge we are going to write a program that generates a description of a Gruffalo. Each time the program is run, a new description will be generated.

By completing this challenge we are going to improve our skills at:

- Using lists and accessing values of a list randomly,
- Concatenating strings together to create a longer string.

Web Address

http://www.101computing.net/the-gruffalo/

Python Code

```python
1.  #The Gruffalo - www.101Computing.net/the-gruffalo/
2.  import random
3.
4.  adjectiveList = ["sharp", "long", "serrated", "pointed", "acute"]
5.  nounList = ["claws", "nails"]
6.  adjective = random.choice(adjectiveList)
7.  noun = random.choice(nounList)
8.  description = "Who is this creature with " + adjective + " " + noun + "?\n"
9.
10. adjectiveList = ["ferocious","large","horrendous","frightful"]
11. colourList = ["dark green","fiery orange","deep blue", "flaming red"]
12. adjective = random.choice(adjectiveList)
13. colour = random.choice(colourList)
14. description += "He has two " + adjective + " " + colour + " eyes."
15.
16. adjectiveList = ["terrible","atrocious","hideous","terrifying"]
17. colourList = ["evil purple","tangy red","mouldy brown","dingy blue"]
```

```
18. nounList = ["jaws","warts at the end of his nose","prickles
    all over his back"]
19. adjective = random.choice(adjectiveList)
20. noun = random.choice(nounList)
21. colour = random.choice(colourList)
22. description += "He has " + adjective + " " + colour + " " +
    noun + ". \n"
23.
24. print(description)
```

48. Lottery Numbers

In this challenge we are going to write a Python program that automatically generates six random numbers (from 1 to 50) and displays them on the screen, sorted in ascending order. The program will need to make sure that each number is unique; the same number cannot come twice in the selection of six selected numbers.

We will complete this code by asking the end-user to type six numbers between 1 and 50. Our code will then count and display the number of matches by comparing the user's six numbers with the six randomly generated lottery numbers!

Web Address

http://www.101computing.net/lottery-numbers/

Python Code

```
1.  #Lottery Numbers - www.101computing.net/lottery-numbers
2.  import random
3.
4.  #1 - Ask the user for their selection of 6 numbers
5.  userNumbers = []
6.  for i in range(0,6):
7.      number = int(input("Enter a number between 1 to 50"))
8.      userNumbers.append(number)
9.
10. #2 - Generate the 6 random numbers
```

```
11. lotteryNumbers = []
12. for i in range (0,6):
13.    number = random.randint(1,50)
14.    #Check if this number has already been picked and ...
15.    while number in lotteryNumbers:
16.        # ... if it has, pick a new number instead
17.        number = random.randint(1,50)
18.
19.    #Now that we have a unique number, let's append it to our
    list.
20.    lotteryNumbers.append(number)
21.
22. #Sort the list in ascending order
23. lotteryNumbers.sort()
24.
25. #Display the list on screen:
26. print("\n>>> Today's lottery numbers are: ")
27. print(lotteryNumbers)
28.
29. #3 - Count the number of matches
30. count = 0
31. for number in userNumbers:
32.    if number in lotteryNumbers:
33.        count += 1
34.
35. print("\n>>> Number of matches: " + str(count))
```

49. Blackjack Challenge

In this challenge we are going to create a Blackjack
game for one player. The computer will be the dealer.

Rules of the game

"Blackjack, also known as twenty-one, is the most widely played casino
banking game in the world. Blackjack is a comparing card game between a
player and dealer, meaning that players compete against the dealer but
not against any other players. It is played with one or more decks of 52
cards. The object of the game is to beat the dealer, which can be done in a
number of ways:

- Get 21 points on the player's first two cards (called a blackjack), without a dealer blackjack;
- Reach a final score higher than the dealer without exceeding 21;
- Let the dealer draw additional cards until his or her hand exceeds

The player or players are dealt an initial two-card hand and add together the value of their cards. Face cards (kings, queens, and jacks) are counted as ten points. A player and the dealer can count his or her own ace as 1 point or 11 points. All other cards are counted as the numeric value shown on the card. After receiving their initial two cards, players have the option of getting a "hit", or taking an additional card. In a given round, the player or the dealer wins by having a score of 21 or by having the highest score that is less than 21. Scoring higher than 21 (called "busting" or "going bust") results in a loss. A player may win by having any final score equal to or less than 21 if the dealer busts. If a player holds an ace valued as 11, the hand is called "soft", meaning that the player cannot go bust by taking an additional card; 11 plus the value of any other card will always be less than or equal to 21. Otherwise, the hand is "hard".

The dealer has to take hits until his or her cards total 17 or more points. (In some casinos the dealer also hits on a "soft" 17, e.g. an initial ace and six.) Players win if they do not bust and have a total that is higher than the dealer's. The dealer loses if he or she busts or has a lesser hand than the player who has not busted. If the player and dealer have the same total, this is called a "push" and the player typically does not win or lose money on that hand."

We will recreate this game for one player only. The end-user will play against the computer (the dealer). Our game will use a text-based interface. Cards will be displayed as follows:

♠ As (Ace of spade), 2s, 3s, ... 9s, 10s, Js, Qs, Ks

♥ Ah (Ace of heart), 2h, 3h, ... 9h, 10h, Jh, Qh, Kh

♣ Ac (Ace of club), 2c, 3c, ... 9c, 10c, Jc, Qc, Kc

♦ Ad (Ace of diamond), 2d, 3d, ... 9d, 10d, Jd, Qd, Kd

Python Code

```
1.  #Blackjack Game - www.101computing.net/blackjack-
    challenge/
2.  import random
3.
4.  def placeBet(playerAmount):
5.      validBet=False
6.      while validBet==False:
7.          print("You currently have $" + str(playerAmount))
8.          #Only accept a whole number for the bet value (integer)

9.          try:
10.            bet = int(input("How much would like to bet?"))
11.         except ValueError:
12.             print("You must enter an integer.\n")
13.         else:
14.            #Can the player afford this bet?
15.            if bet > playerAmount:
16.                print("You do not have enough money for this bet.")

17.                print("You should place a lower bet.")
18.            elif bet < 1:
19.                print("You need to bet at least $1.\n")
20.            else:
21.                validBet=True
22.     return bet
23.
24. def getHandValue(hand):
25.     global deck
26.     global deckValue
27.     total=0
28.
29.     #Add up the value of each card in the hand
30.     for card in hand:
31.         total+=deckValue[card]
32.
33.     #If total > 21, check if hte hand includes any aces that c
        an be changed from 11 points to 1 point
34.     if total > 21:
35.         for card in hand:
36.             if card in ["Ah","As","Ad","Ac"]:
37.                 total -= 10
38.                 if total<=21:
39.                     break
```

113

```
40.     #Return total value
41.     return total
42.
43. playerAmount=100
44. deck=["Ah","2h","3h","4h","5h","6h","7h","8h","9h","10h","Jh
    ","Qh","Kh","As","2s","3s","4s","5s","6s","7s","8s","9s","10
    s","Js","Qs","Ks","Ad","2d","3d","4d","5d","6d","7d","8d","9
    d","10d","Jd","Qd","Kd","Ac","2c","3c","4c","5c","6c","7c","
    8c","9c","10c","Jc","Qc","Kc"]
45. deckValue={"Ah":11,"2h":2,"3h":3,"4h":4,"5h":5,"6h":6,"7h":7
    ,"8h":8,"9h":9,"10h":10,"Jh":10,"Qh":10,"Kh":10,"As":11,"2s"
    :2,"3s":3,"4s":4,"5s":5,"6s":6,"7s":7,"8s":8,"9s":9,"10s":10
    ,"Js":10,"Qs":10,"Ks":10,"Ad":11,"2d":2,"3d":3,"4d":4,"5d":5
    ,"6d":6,"7d":7,"8d":8,"9d":9,"10d":10,"Jd":10,"Qd":10,"Kd":1
    0,"Ac":11,"2c":2,"3c":3,"4c":4,"5c":5,"6c":6,"7c":7,"8c":8,"
    9c":9,"10c":10,"Jc":10,"Qc":10,"Kc":10}
46.
47. while playerAmount>0:
48.     print("--------------------")
49.     bet = placeBet(playerAmount)
50.     playerHand=[]
51.     dealerHand=[]
52.     playerTotal = 0
53.     dealerTotal = 0
54.     currentCardIndex=0
55.
56.     random.shuffle(deck)
57.
58.     #Dealer's Hand
59.     dealerHand.append(deck[currentCardIndex])
60.     currentCardIndex+=1
61.     dealerHand.append(deck[currentCardIndex])
62.     currentCardIndex+=1
63.     dealerTotal=getHandValue(dealerHand)
64.
65.     #Will the dealer hand include more cards?
66.     while True:
67.         if dealerTotal<17:
68.             dealerHand.append(deck[currentCardIndex])
69.             currentCardIndex+=1
70.             dealerTotal=getHandValue(dealerHand)
71.         elif dealerTotal>=17:
72.             break
73.
74.     #Player's Hand
75.     print("Your Hand:")
76.     print(deck[currentCardIndex])
77.     playerHand.append(deck[currentCardIndex])
78.     currentCardIndex+=1
```

```
79.    print(deck[currentCardIndex])
80.    playerHand.append(deck[currentCardIndex])
81.    currentCardIndex+=1
82.    playerTotal=getHandValue(playerHand)
83.    print("Your total: " + str(playerTotal))
84.
85.    #Give the player the option to add extra cards (hit) or to
       stand
86.    while playerTotal<21:
87.      choice=""
88.      while choice!="hit" and choice!="stand":
89.          choice=input("Would you like to hit or stand?").lowe
       r()
90.
91.      if choice=="hit":
92.          print(deck[currentCardIndex])
93.        playerHand.append(deck[currentCardIndex])
94.        currentCardIndex+=1
95.        playerTotal=getHandValue(playerHand)
96.        print("Your total: "+str(playerTotal))
97.      elif choice=="stand":
98.        break
99.
100.     #Reveals the Dealer's Hand
101.   print("Dealer's Hand:")
102.   for card in dealerHand:
103.     print(card)
104.   print("Dealer's Total: " + str(dealerTotal))
105.
106.   #Find out who wins this game!
107.   print("")
108.   if playerTotal>dealerTotal and playerTotal<=21:
109.     print("You Win!!")
110.     playerAmount += bet
111.     print("You now have $" + str(playerAmount))
112.   elif playerTotal>21 and dealerTotal>21:
113.     print("Both the dealer and you went bust.")
114.     print("No gain - No loss.")
115.     print("You still have $" + str(playerAmount))
116.   elif playerTotal>21:
117.     print("You have gone bust!!")
118.     playerAmount -= bet
119.     print("You now have $" + str(playerAmount))
120.   elif dealerTotal>21:
121.     print("The dealer has gone bust. You win!!")
122.     playerAmount += bet
123.     print("You now have $" + str(playerAmount))
124.   elif playerTotal == dealerTotal:
125.     print("You push - No gain - No loss.")
```

```
126.      print("You still have $" + str(playerAmount))
127.  else:
128.      print "The Dealer Wins. You lose!"
129.      playerAmount -= bet
130.      print("You now have $" + str(playerAmount))
131.
132.  #Check if the player wants to carry on playing
133.  if playerAmount>0:
134.      carryOn=""
135.      while carryOn!="yes" and carryOn!="no":
136.          carryOn = input("Do you want to continue? (yes/no)").l
     ower()
137.      if carryOn=="no":
138.          print("Good Bye!")
139.          break
140.
141.if playerAmount==0:
142.    print("Sorry you have now spent all your money! Good bye f
     or now!")
```

50. Battleship Challenge

For this challenge we are not going to recreate a full battleship game. Instead we are going to focus on randomly placing the ships on the grid using an algorithm.

Our code will use Python Turtle to draw the full grid. The grid is a 10 by 10 array. As Python does not support 2-dimensional arrays, we will create a list of list instead. The grid will first be initialised with the value 0 in each cell of the array. To place a ship we will change the value from 0 to 1 on all the required cells.

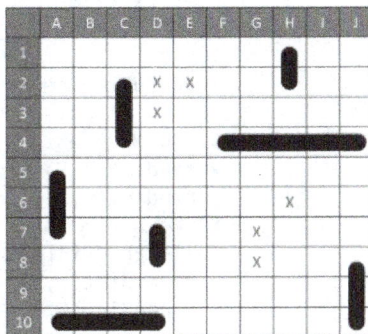

This program will use four functions called:

- *addSubmarine()* to place a submarine (ship of size 1) on the grid.

- *addDestroyer()* to place a destroyer (ship of size 2) on the grid.
- *addCruiser()* to place a cruiser (ship of size 3) on the grid.
- *addAircraftCarrier()* to place an aircraft carrier (ship of size 4) on the grid.

Note that when placing a destroyer, cruiser or aircraft carrier, we can either place it horizontally or vertically. However before placing the ship on the grid we must ensure that:
- All the cells used to place the ship are empty (No conflict with another ship on the grid),
- The ship will not go off the 10 by 10 grid.

Web Address

http://www.101computing.net/battleship-challenge/

Python Code

```
1.  #Battleship Challenge - 101computing.net/battleship-
    challenge
2.  import turtle
3.  from random import randint
4.
5.  myPen = turtle.Turtle()
6.  myPen.tracer(0)
7.  myPen.speed(0)
8.  myPen.color("#000000")
9.  topLeft_x=-150
10. topLeft_y=150
11.
12. def addSubmarine(grid):
13.    #Place a submarine on the grid
14.    #A submarine is a small ship of size 1
15.    x=randint(0,9)
16.    y=randint(0,9)
17.    #Check that there is not already a boat at this location
18.    while grid[x][y]!=0:
19.       x=randint(0,9)
20.       y=randint(0,9)
21.    #Add submarine to the grid
22.    grid[x][y]=1
23.
24. def addDestroyer(grid):
25.    #Place a destroyer on the grid
```

```
26.    #A destroyer is a ship of size 2
27.    direction=randint(0,1)
28.    if direction==0: #horizontal
29.       x=randint(0,8)
30.       y=randint(0,9)
31.       while grid[x][y]!=0 or grid[x+1][y]!=0:
32.          x=randint(0,8)
33.          y=randint(0,9)
34.       grid[x][y]=1
35.       grid[x+1][y]=1
36.    else: #vertical
37.       x=randint(0,9)
38.       y=randint(0,8)
39.       while grid[x][y]!=0 or grid[x][y+1]!=0:
40.          x=randint(0,9)
41.          y=randint(0,8)
42.       grid[x][y]=1
43.       grid[x][y+1]=1
44.
45. def addCruiser(grid):
46.    #Place a cruiser on the grid
47.    #A cruiser is a ship of size 3
48.    direction=randint(0,1)
49.    if direction==0: #horizontal
50.       x=randint(0,7)
51.       y=randint(0,9)
52.       while grid[x][y]!=0 or grid[x+1][y]!=0 or grid[x+2][y]!=
   0:
53.          x=randint(0,7)
54.          y=randint(0,9)
55.       grid[x][y]=1
56.       grid[x+1][y]=1
57.       grid[x+2][y]=1
58.    else: #vertical
59.       x=randint(0,9)
60.       y=randint(0,7)
61.       while grid[x][y]!=0 or grid[x][y+1]!=0 or grid[x][y+2]!=
   0:
62.          x=randint(0,9)
63.          y=randint(0,7)
64.       grid[x][y]=1
65.       grid[x][y+1]=1
66.       grid[x][y+2]=1
67.
68. def addAircraftCarrier(grid):
69.    #Place an aircraft carrier on the grid
70.    #An aircraft carrier is a large ship of size 4
71.    direction=randint(0,1)
72.    if direction==0: #horizontal
```

```
73.      x=randint(0,6)
74.      y=randint(0,9)
75.      while grid[x][y]!=0 or grid[x+1][y]!=0 or grid[x+2][y]!=
    0 or grid[x+2][y]!=0:
76.        x=randint(0,6)
77.        y=randint(0,9)
78.      grid[x][y]=1
79.      grid[x+1][y]=1
80.      grid[x+2][y]=1
81.      grid[x+3][y]=1
82.    else: #vertical
83.      x=randint(0,9)
84.      y=randint(0,6)
85.      while grid[x][y]!=0 or grid[x][y+1]!=0 or grid[x][y+2]!=
    0 or grid[x][y+3]!=0:
86.        x=randint(0,9)
87.        y=randint(0,6)
88.      grid[x][y]=1
89.      grid[x][y+1]=1
90.      grid[x][y+2]=1
91.      grid[x][y+3]=1
92.
93. def drawGrid(intDim):
94.   for i in range(0,11):
95.     myPen.penup()
96.     myPen.goto(topLeft_x,topLeft_y-i*intDim)
97.     myPen.pendown()
98.     myPen.goto(topLeft_x+10*intDim,topLeft_y-i*intDim)
99.   for i in range(0,11):
100.    myPen.penup()
101.    myPen.goto(topLeft_x+i*intDim,topLeft_y)
102.    myPen.pendown()
103.    myPen.goto(topLeft_x+i*intDim,topLeft_y-10*intDim)
104.  for i in range(0,10):
105.    myPen.penup()
106.    myPen.goto(topLeft_x+i*intDim+10,topLeft_y+10)
107.    myPen.write(chr(65+i))
108.  for i in range(1,11):
109.    myPen.penup()
110.    myPen.goto(topLeft_x-15,topLeft_y-i*intDim+10)
111.    myPen.write(str(i))
112.
113.  myPen.setheading(0)
114.  myPen.goto(topLeft_x,topLeft_y-intDim)
115.  for row in range (0,10):
116.    for column in range (0,10):
117.        if grid[column][row]>0:
118.          box(intDim)
119.          myPen.penup()
```

```
120.            myPen.forward(intDim)
121.            myPen.pendown()
122.       myPen.setheading(270)
123.       myPen.penup()
124.       myPen.forward(intDim)
125.       myPen.setheading(180)
126.       myPen.forward(intDim*10)
127.       myPen.setheading(0)
128.       myPen.pendown()
129.
130.# This function draws a box by drawing each side of the squa
    re and using the fill function
131.def box(intDim):
132.       myPen.begin_fill()
133.       # 0 deg.
134.       myPen.forward(intDim)
135.       myPen.left(90)
136.       # 90 deg.
137.       myPen.forward(intDim)
138.       myPen.left(90)
139.       # 180 deg.
140.       myPen.forward(intDim)
141.       myPen.left(90)
142.       # 270 deg.
143.       myPen.forward(intDim)
144.       myPen.end_fill()
145.       myPen.setheading(0)
146.
147.############ MAIN PROGRAM STARTS HERE ############
148.#initialise empty 10 by 10 grid
149.grid    = [[0,0,0,0,0,0,0,0,0,0]]
150.grid.append([0,0,0,0,0,0,0,0,0,0])
151.grid.append([0,0,0,0,0,0,0,0,0,0])
152.grid.append([0,0,0,0,0,0,0,0,0,0])
153.grid.append([0,0,0,0,0,0,0,0,0,0])
154.grid.append([0,0,0,0,0,0,0,0,0,0])
155.grid.append([0,0,0,0,0,0,0,0,0,0])
156.grid.append([0,0,0,0,0,0,0,0,0,0])
157.grid.append([0,0,0,0,0,0,0,0,0,0])
158.grid.append([0,0,0,0,0,0,0,0,0,0])
159.
160.addSubmarine(grid) #Place submarine on the grid
161.addDestroyer(grid) #Place first destroyer on the grid
162.addDestroyer(grid) #Place second destroyer on the grid
163.addCruiser(grid) #Place first cruiser on the grid
164.addCruiser(grid) #Place second cruiser on the grid
165.addAircraftCarrier(grid) #Place aircraft carrier destroyer o
    n the grid
166.
```

```
167. drawGrid(25) #25 is the width of each square on the grid
168. myPen.getscreen().update()
```

51. NATO Phonetic Alphabet

The NATO Phonetic Alphabet is the most widely used spelling alphabet. A spelling alphabet (aka radio alphabet or telephone alphabet) is a set of words used to stand for the letters of an alphabet in oral communication. Each word in the spelling alphabet typically replaces the name of the letter with which it starts. It is used to spell out words when speaking to someone not able to see the speaker, or when the audio channel is not clear.

Nowadays people may use the NATO Phonetic alphabet when they have to spell their name or their postcode over the phone. For instance, the name Smith would spell Sierra – Mike – India – Tango – Hotel.

This challenge consists of writing a computer program that will ask the end-user to enter their last name. The program will output their last name using the NATO Phonetic Alphabet.

Web Address

http://www.101computing.net/nato-phonetic-alphabet/

Python Code

```
1.  #NATO Phonetic Alphabet - www.101Computing.net/nato-
    phonetic
2.
3.  #Use a Python Dictionary to store the NATO phonetic alphabet
4.  alphabet = {"A":"Alpha","B":"Beta","C":"Charlie","D":"Delta"
    ,"E":"Echo","F":"Foxstrot","G":"Golf","H":"Hotel","I":"India
    ","J":"Juliett","K":"Kilo","L":"Lima","M":"Mike","N":"Novemb
    er","O":"Oscar","P":"Papa","Q":"Quebec","R":"Romeo","S":"Sie
    rra","T":"Tango","U":"Uniform","V":"Victor","W":"Whiskey","X
    ":"X-Ray","Y":"Yankee","Z":"Zulu" }
5.
6.  name = input("Enter your lastname:").upper()
```

```
7.
8.  print("Converting lastname using NATO Phonetic Alphabet:")
9.
10. for character in name:
11.    #Check if it's a letter from the alphabet
12.    if character in alphabet:
13.       print(alphabet[character])
14.    else:
15.       print(character)
```

52. Morse Code Decoder

The aim of this challenge is to create a Morse code
converter that lets the user enter any message. The
program should then display the message in Morse
code. Morse code is a method of transmitting text information as a series
of on-off tones, lights, or clicks that can be directly understood by a skilled
listener or observer without special equipment.

Each character (letter or numeral) is represented by a unique sequence of
dots and dashes. The duration of a dash is three times the duration of a
dot.

For this challenge we will be using the international Morse code as
follows:

International Morse Code

1. The length of a dot is one unit.
2. A dash is three units.
3. The space between parts of the same letter is one unit.
4. The space between letters is three units.
5. The space between words is seven units.

A ● ▬
B ▬ ● ● ●
C ▬ ● ▬ ●
D ▬ ● ●
E ●
F ● ● ▬ ●
G ▬ ▬ ●
H ● ● ● ●
I ● ●
J ● ▬ ▬ ▬
K ▬ ● ▬
L ● ▬ ● ●
M ▬ ▬
N ▬ ●
O ▬ ▬ ▬
P ● ▬ ▬ ●
Q ▬ ▬ ● ▬
R ● ▬ ●
S ● ● ●
T ▬

U ● ● ▬
V ● ● ● ▬
W ● ▬ ▬
X ▬ ● ● ▬
Y ▬ ● ▬ ▬
Z ▬ ▬ ● ●

1 ● ▬ ▬ ▬ ▬
2 ● ● ▬ ▬ ▬
3 ● ● ● ▬ ▬
4 ● ● ● ● ▬
5 ● ● ● ● ●
6 ▬ ● ● ● ●
7 ▬ ▬ ● ● ●
8 ▬ ▬ ▬ ● ●
9 ▬ ▬ ▬ ▬ ●
0 ▬ ▬ ▬ ▬ ▬

Web Address

http://www.101computing.net/morse-code-encoder/

Python Code:

```
1.  #Morse Code Encode/Decoder - 101computing.net/morse-code-
    encoder/
2.
3.  #First let's store the morse code for the alphabet using a d
    ictionary
4.  morseCode = {"A":".-","B":"-...","C":"-.-."}
5.  morseCode["D"] = "-.."
6.  morseCode["E"] = "."
7.  morseCode["F"] = "..-."
8.  morseCode["G"] = "--."
9.  morseCode["H"] = "...."
10. morseCode["I"] = ".."
11. morseCode["J"] = ".---"
12. morseCode["K"] = "-.-"
```

```
13. morseCode["L"] = ".-.."
14. morseCode["M"] = "--"
15. morseCode["N"] = "-."
16. morseCode["O"] = "---"
17. morseCode["P"] = ".--."
18. morseCode["Q"] = "--.-"
19. morseCode["R"] = ".-."
20. morseCode["S"] = "..."
21. morseCode["T"] = "-"
22. morseCode["U"] = "..-"
23. morseCode["V"] = "...-"
24. morseCode["W"] = ".--"
25. morseCode["X"] = "-..-"
26. morseCode["Y"] = "-.--"
27. morseCode["Z"] = "--.."
28. #Digits from 0 to 9
29. morseCode["1"] = ".----"
30. morseCode["2"] = "..---"
31. morseCode["3"] = "...--"
32. morseCode["4"] = "....-"
33. morseCode["5"] = "....."
34. morseCode["6"] = "-...."
35. morseCode["7"] = "--..."
36. morseCode["8"] = "---.."
37. morseCode["9"] = "----."
38. morseCode["0"] = "-----"
39.
40. option = input("Press 1 to encode a message in Morse code, 2
    to decode a Morse code message.")
41. if option=="1":
42.    #Retrieve end-
    user's message and convert it to upper case.
43.    message = input("Type a message to convert in morse code (
    e.g. \"SOS\"?)").upper()
44.    encodedMessage = ""
45.
46.    #Convert each letter into morse code:
47.    for character in message:
48.      #Check that the character is in the moreCode dictionary
    (e.g letter of the alphabet)
49.      if character in morseCode:
50.        encodedMessage += morseCode[character] + " "
51.      else:
52.        #Replace unrecognised characters with a space
53.        encodedMessage += " "
54.
55.    #Display the message in morse code:
56.    print("Your message in morse code is:")
57.    print(encodedMessage)
```

```
58.
59. elif option=="2":
60.    #Inverse the dictionary
61.    inverseMorseCode = {key: value for value, key in morseCode
       .items()}
62.
63.    #Retrieve end-user's Morse code
64.    morseCodeMessage = input("Type a Morse code sequence to de
       code (e.g. \"... --- ...\"?)")
65.    morseCodes = morseCodeMessage.split(" ")
66.    decodedMessage = ""
67.
68.    #Convert each letter into morse code:
69.    for code in morseCodes:
70.       #Check that the character is in the moreCode dictionary
       (e.g letter of the alphabet)
71.       if code in inverseMorseCode:
72.          decodedMessage += inverseMorseCode[code]
73.       else:
74.          #Replace unrecognised characters with a space
75.          decodedMessage += " "
76.
77.    #Display the message:
78.    print("Your message is:")
79.    print(decodedMessage)
80.
81. else:
82.    print("Invalid option!")
```

Chapter #6: String Manipulation Techniques

In nearly all of the challenges we have completed so far we have used variables to store **string** values. We have already used some string manipulation techniques such as **string concatenation** (joining strings together) and **string casting** (e.g. casting an integer or float to a string and vice-versa). Remember a string is a collection (list) of **characters**. So using a string is similar to using a list. You can hence reuse some of the techniques covered in the previous chapter to your string variables.

Other techniques can be used to change the **case** of a string (lower case, upper case, title case), extract characters from a string (in python this is called **slicing**), loop through all the characters of a string one at a time, convert characters of a string using the **ASCII code** and concatenate (join) two strings together.

The next few challenges will help you further improve your string manipulation techniques including:

- String Concatenation,
- String Casting,
- Changing the Case of a String,
- Slicing Strings,
- Using the ASCII Code.

53. ASCII Art Banner

Look at the ASCII banner below. For this challenge we want the user to enter their name and the computer to generate an ASCII banner using their name ("Hello" + name).

```
          \|||||/
          ( O O )
|--oOo-----(_)-----------|
|                        |
|     Hello World!        |
|                        |
|------------------Ooo---|
      |__||__|
       ||  ||
      oOO  Ooo
```

We need to make sure that the ASCII banner takes into consideration the number of characters in the user's name to make sure it always looks fine with the message being centred inside the banner.

Web Address

http://www.101computing.net/string-manipulation-ascii-art/

Python Code

```
1.  #ASCII Art Banner - www.101computing.net/string-
    manipulation-ascii-art/
2.
3.  name=input("What's your name?")
4.
5.  lengthName = len(name)
6.  spacesLeft = (18 - lengthName) // 2
7.
8.  if (18 - lengthName) % 2 == 1:
9.    spacesRight = spacesLeft + 1
10. else:
11.   spacesRight = spacesLeft
12.
13. print("\n")
14. print("          \|||||/          ")
15. print("          ( O O )          ")
16. print("|--oOo-----(_)-----------|")
17. print("|                        |")
18. print("|" + (spacesLeft * " ") + "Hello " + name + (spacesRight * " ") + "|")
19. print("|                        |")
20. print("|------------------Ooo---|")
21. print("      |__||__|          ")
22. print("       ||  ||          ")
23. print("      oOO  Ooo          ")
```

54. Number Plate Generator

By completing this challenge we are going to learn how to use ASCII code when manipulating strings. We will use the *chr()* and *ord()* python instructions to convert characters into ASCII code and vice versa. For instance 65 is the ASCII code for character "A", so:

- *chr(65)* returns the letter "A",
- *ord("A")* returns the number 65.

Our first challenge consists of creating a program that generates a random plate number each time it is run. The plate number will have to adhere to this format:

2 UPPER CASE LETTERS followed by 2 digits (0 to 9) followed by a space followed by 3 UPPER CASE LETTERS.

CS15 NET

101Computing.net

Web Address

http://www.101computing.net/number-plate-generator/

Python Code

```
1.  #Number PLate Generator - www.101computing.net/number-plate-
    generator/
2.  from random import randint
3.
4.  #Generate a random Uppercase letter (based on ASCII code)
5.  # 65 -> A to 90 -> Z
6.  upperCaseLetter2=chr(randint(65,90))
7.  upperCaseLetter1=chr(randint(65,90))
8.  randomnumber1=chr(randint(48,57))
9.  randomnumber2=chr(randint(48,57))
10. upperCaseLetter3=chr(randint(65,90))
11. upperCaseLetter4=chr(randint(65,90))
12. upperCaseLetter5=chr(randint(65,90))
```

```
13.
14. print(upperCaseLetter1 + upperCaseLetter2 + randomnumber1 +
    randomnumber2 + " " + upperCaseLetter3 + upperCaseLetter4 +
    upperCaseLetter5)
```

55. Number Plate Validation

For this challenge we will write a program that will ask the user to enter an eight-digit UK number plate. The program will then confirm whether the number plate is valid or not.

Remember, a valid number plate has to follow this format:
2 UPPER CASE LETTERS followed by 2 digits (0 to 9) followed by a space
followed by 3 UPPER CASE LETTERS

Web Address
http://www.101computing.net/number-plate-generator/

Python Code

```
1.  #Number Plate Validation - www.101computing.net/number-
    plate-generator/
2.  print("---------------------------------------")
3.  print("- welcome to the number plate validator -")
4.  print("---------------------------------------")
5.
6.  valid=True
7.  yourPlate=input("Input a number plate number")
8.
9.  #It it 8 characters long?
10. if len(yourPlate)!=8:
11.     valid=False
12. else:
13.    # Does it start with 2 UPPERCASE letters?
14.    for i in range(0,2):
15.      if not(ord(yourPlate[i]) >= 65 and ord(yourPlate[i]) <=
    90):
16.            valid=False
17.
18.    # Followed by 2 numbers?
```

```
19.   for i in range(2,4):
20.      if not(ord(yourPlate[i]) >= 48 and ord(yourPlate[i]) <=
      57):
21.            valid=False
22.
23.   #Followed by a space
24.   if ord(yourPlate[4]) != 32:
25.      valid=False
26.
27.   # Followed by 3 UPPERCASE letters?
28.   for i in range(5,8):
29.      if not(ord(yourPlate[i]) >= 65 and ord(yourPlate[i]) <=
      90):
30.            valid=False
31.
32. #Final Output
33. if valid == True:
34.      print("This number plate is valid.")
35. else:
36.      print("This number plate is invalid.")
```

56. HTML Code Builder

In this challenge, we are going to create a Python program to help us generate HTML code to create bullet point lists in HTML as well as tables. This HTML code could then be used inside a webpage.

HTML Lists:
In HTML you can create bullet point lists to display information on the page. To do so you need to use both a <UL> tag to open and close the list and a <LI> tag for each bullet point within the list. Here is HTML the code for a list containing three bullet points:

```
<UL>
      <LI>First bullet point,</LI>
      <LI>Second bullet point,</LI>
      <LI>and so on...</LI>
</UL>
```

HTML Tables:

From time to time, when building a webpage in HTML, you need to present your data using a table. A table (<TABLE>) is made of rows (<TR>). Each row is made of data cells (<TD>).

So for instance a 3×2 table contains 3 rows and each row contains 2 data cells. The HTML code of such a table is as follows:

Our aim is to write a python program to prompt the user to enter the number of bullet points they need in their HTML list as well as the number of rows and the number of columns they need for their table. The program should then generate the HTML code for the required list and for the required table.

Web Address

http://www.101computing.net/html-code-builder-in-python/

Python Code

```
1.  #HTML Code Builder - www.101computing.net/html-code-builder-
    in-python
2.
3.  #HTML Lists
4.  numberOfBulletPoints = int(input("How many bullet points do
    you need?"))
5.
6.  HTMLCode = "<UL>"
7.  for i in range(0,numberOfBulletPoints):
8.      HTMLCode = HTMLCode + "\n" + "   <LI>...</LI>"
9.
10. HTMLCode = HTMLCode + "\n" + "</UL>"
```

```
11. print("Here is the HTML code for your list of bullet points:
    ")
12. print(HTMLCode)
13.
14. #HTML Tables
15. numberOfRows = int(input("How many rows do you need in your
    table?"))
16. numberOfColumns = int(input("How many columns do you need in
    your table?"))
17.
18. HTMLCode = "<TABLE>\n"
19. for r in range(0,numberOfRows):
20.    HTMLCode = HTMLCode + "    <TR>"
21.    for c in range(0,numberOfColumns):
22.       HTMLCode = HTMLCode + "<TD>...</TD>"
23.    HTMLCode = HTMLCode + "</TR>\n"
24. HTMLCode = HTMLCode + "</TABLE>"
25.
26. print("Here is the HTML code for your HTML table:")
27. print(HTMLCode)
```

57. What's My Username?

In this challenge we will write a program that asks the end-user to enter the following information:
- Firstname,
- Lastname,
- Year Group.

The program will then use string manipulation techniques to generate the end-user's username using the following rules:
- 2-digit year group + first letter of firstname + lastname.
- The username should be all lowercase.
- If the year group is in 1 digit only (e.g.: 7) then add a "0" in front to make it two digits e.g. "07".

For instance:

Firstname	Lastname	Year Group	Expected Output (Username)
John	Lennon	7	07jlennon
Paul	McCartney	11	11pmccartney
George	Harrison	8	08gharrison
Ringo	Starr	9	09rstarr

Web Address
http://www.101computing.net/whats-my-username/

Python Code

```
1.  #What's My Username - www.101computing.net/whats-my-
    username/
2.
3.  #Retrieve and validate user inputs:
4.  firstname = input("Type your firstname:")
5.  while firstname=="":
6.    firstname = input("Invalid firstname - Try again:")
7.
8.  lastname = input("Type your lastname:")
9.  while lastname=="":
10.   lastname = input("Invalid lastname - Try again:")
11.
12. yearGroup = input("Your Year Group?")
13. while not yearGroup in ["7","8","9","10","11"]:
14.   yearGroup = input("Invalid Year Group - Try again:")
15.
16. #Process Data
17. if len(yearGroup)==1:
18.   yearGroup = "0" + yearGroup
19.
20. initial = firstname[0].lower()
21. username = yearGroup + initial + lastname.lower()
22.
23. #Output
24. print("Your username is: " + username)
```

58. Password Checker

For this challenge we will write a program where the end-user has to type a password. The program will then return a score to tell the end-user how secure their password is. The score will be based on the following criteria:

Criteria	Score
The password is at least 8 characters long.	+5pts
The password contains number and letters.	+10pts
The password contains at least one punctuation sign.	+5pts
The password contains lowercase and uppercase characters.	+10pts

Web Address
http://www.101computing.net/password-checker/

Python Code

```
1.  #Password Checker - www.101computing.net/password-checker/
2.
3.  password = input("Type your password:")
4.
5.  #Check the password for specific characters
6.  lowercase = False
7.  for c in password:
8.    if c in "abcdefghijklmnopqrstuvwxyz":
9.      lowercase = True
10.
11. uppercase = False
12. for c in password:
13.   if c in "ABCDEFGHIJKLMNOPQRSTUVWXYZ":
14.     uppercase = True
15.
16. if uppercase==True or lowercase==True:
17.   letter=True
18. else:
19.   letter=False
20.
```

```
21. digit = False
22. for c in password:
23.     if c in "1234567890":
24.         digit = True
25.
26. punctuation = False
27. for c in password:
28.     if c in "!£$%^&*()-_=+][}{#~'@;:\|,.<>/?*":
29.         punctuation = True
30.
31. #Calculate the security score of the password
32. score=0
33. message=""
34.
35. if len(password)<8:
36.     message = message + "Your password should be at least 8 ch
    aracters long.\n"
37. else:
38.     score = score + 5
39.
40. if lowercase==False or uppercase==False:
41.     message = message + "Your password should contain both low
    ercase and uppercase characters.\n"
42. else:
43.     score = score + 10
44.
45. if digit==False or letter==False:
46.     message = message + "Your password should contain both let
    ters and digits from 0 to 9.\n"
47. else:
48.     score = score + 10
49.
50. if punctuation==False:
51.     message = message + "Your password should contain at least
    one punctuation sign.\n"
52. else:
53.     score = score + 5
54.
55. #Output socre and recoomendations to the user
56. print("Your security score is " + str(score) + ".")
57. if message!="":
58.     print("To make your password stronger you should consider
    the following options:")
59.     print(message)
```

59. E-Mail Address Validation

The aim of this challenge is to write a computer program that asks the end-user to type their e-mail address. The program should decide whether the e-mail being entered is a valid one or not.

Some of the validation checks that our program will complete are as follows:
- The email should contain one and only one "@" sign.
- The email should contain at least one "." sign located after the "@" sign. However it may contains more than one "." (e.g. for emails ending in ".co.uk")
- The email cannot contain any space or "#" characters.
- The "@" sign cannot be in the first position and there should be at least 2 characters between the "@" and the ".".
- The email cannot end with a ".".

Though it would be possible to complete this challenge using a regular expression, we have decided to use a range of string manipulation techniques instead.

Web Address

http://www.101computing.net/my-e-mail-validation-script/

Find out more about Regular Expressions:

https://docs.python.org/2/library/re.html

Python Code

```
1. #E-mail address validation - www.101computing.net/my-e-mail-
   validation-script/
2.
3. #A function to check if an email address seems valid or not

4. def checkEmail(email):
5.     atSignPosition=-1
6.     dotSignPosition=-1
```

```
7.    validEmail = True
8.
9.    #Check for invalid Characters
10.   if " " in email or "#" in email:
11.       print("Invalid characters used in e-mail address.")
12.       return False
13.
14.   #Check for number and position of @ sign
15.   if email.count("@")!=1:
16.       print("An email address must contain one and only one '@
      ' sign.")
17.       return False
18.
19.   atSignPosition = email.find("@")
20.   if atSignPosition==0:
21.       print("An email cannot start with an '@' sign.")
22.       return False
23.
24.   #check for presence and positin of "." in the domain exten
      sion (e.g. .com or .co.uk)
25.   dotPosition = email.find(".",atSignPosition)
26.   if dotPosition-atSignPosition<2:
27.       print("The name server should be at least two characters
      long.")
28.       return False
29.
30.   if email[len(email)-1]==".":
31.       print("An e-mail address cannot end with a '.'")
32.       return False
33.
34.   #If we have reached this line, we have passed all checks!

35.   return True
36.
37. email=input("Type your e-mail address:")
38.
39. #Ouput final decision
40. if checkEmail(email) == True:
41.       print("This seems to be a valid e-mail address.")
42. else:
43.       print("This is not a valid e-mail address.")
```

137

60. Word Score Challenge

```
If
A B C D E F G H I J K L M N O P Q R S T U V W X Y Z

Equals
1 2 3 4 5 6 7 8 9 10 11 12 13 14 15 16 17 18 19 20 21 22 23 24 25 26

Then
K  N  O  W  L  E  D  G  E
11 + 14 + 15 + 23 + 12 + 5 + 4 + 7 + 5  = 96%

And
H  A  R  D  W  O  R  K
8 + 1 + 18 + 4 + 23 + 15 + 18 + 11  = 98%

Both are important, but fall just short of 100%

But
A  T  T  I  T  U  D  E
1 + 20 + 20 + 9 + 20 + 21 + 4 + 5 = 100%
```

In this challenge we will write a Python script that will prompt the end-user to enter a word, e.g. "Hello". The script will then calculate the score of this word using the letter values (A=1, B=2, C=3…).

Web Address

http://www.101computing.net/word-score-challenge/

Python Code

```python
1.  #Word Score Challenge - www.101computing.net/word-score-
    challenge/
2.  word = input("Type a word").upper()
3.
4.  wordScore=0
5.  addition=""
6.
7.  for letter in word:
8.    # Considering that the ASCCI code for "A" is 65
9.    letterValue=ord(letter) - 64
10.   if (addition==""):
11.     addition = str(letterValue)
12.   else:
13.     addition = addition + " + " + str(letterValue)
14.   wordScore += letterValue
15.
16. print(addition + " = " + str(wordScore) + "%")
```

61. Love Match Calculator

For this challenge we will write a program that will prompt the user to enter two first names. The program will then calculate and return a Love Match Score, using the following criteria:

Criteria	Score
Both first names have the same numbers of letters.	+20pts
Both first names start with a vowel.	+10pts
Both first names start with a consonant.	+5pts
Both first names have the same number of vowels.	+12pts
Both first names have the same number of consonants.	+12pts
Both first names contain at least a "l", "o", "v" or "e".	+7pts

Web Address

http://www.101computing.net/love-match-calculator/

Python Code

```
1.  #Love Match Calculator - www.101computing.net/love-match-
    calculator/
2.  print("****************************")
3.  print("*   Love Match Calculator   *")
4.  print("****************************")
5.
6.  #Retrieve User Inputs
7.  name1=input("Type a firstname:")
8.  name2=input("Type another firstname:")
9.  name1=name1.lower()
10. name2=name2.lower()
11.
12. #Initialise key variables
13. score=0
14. vowels=["a","e","i","o","u","y"]
```

```
15. consonants=["b","c","d","f","g","h","j","k","m","n","p","q",
    "r","s","t","v","w","x","z"]
16. vowelsInName1=0
17. vowelsInName2=0
18. consonantsInName1=0
19. consonantsInName2=0
20. containsLoveLetter1=False
21. containsLoveLetter2=False
22.
23. #Check if both names have the same number of characters
24. if len(name1)==len(name2):
25.    score = score + 20
26.
27. #Check if both names start with a vowel
28. if (name1[0] in vowels) and (name2[0] in vowels):
29.     score = score + 10
30.
31. #Check if both names start with a consonant
32. if (name1[0] in consonants) and (name2[0] in consonants):
33.     score = score + 5
34.
35. #Count the number of vowels and consonants in name1
36. for i in range(0,len(name1)):
37.    if name1[i] in vowels:
38.        vowelsInName1=vowelsInName1 + 1
39.    if name1[i] in consonants:
40.        consonantsInName1=consonantsInName1 + 1
41.    if name1[i] in ["l","o","v","e"]:
42.        containsLoveLetter1 = True
43.
44. #Count the number of vowels and consonants in name 2
45. for i in range(0,len(name2)):
46.    if name2[i] in vowels:
47.        vowelsInName2=vowelsInName2 + 1
48.    if name2[i] in consonants:
49.        consonantsInName2=consonantsInName2 + 1
50.    if name2[i] in ["l","o","v","e"]:
51.        containsLoveLetter2 = True
52.
53. #Check if both names have the same number of vowels
54. if vowelsInName1==vowelsInName2:
55.    score = score + 12
56.
57. #Check if both names have the same number of consonants
58. if consonantsInName1==consonantsInName2:
59.    score = score + 12
60.
61. #Both names contain an l or o or v or e
62. if containsLoveLetter1 and containsLoveLetter2:
```

```
63.     score = score + 7
64.
65. #Display final love match score
66. print("Your love match score is: " + str(score))
```

62. Scrabble Challenge

This challenge consists of creating a computer program that displays a random selection of seven letters to the end-user. Each letter is given a value based on the values used in the game of Scrabble.

The user is then asked to enter a word made up using the given letters used in any order. The program should check that the word given by the end-user consists of the right letters and then calculate the score of the word based on the letters used and their values.

For instance the word "CODING" would give a score of 3 + 1 + 2 + 1 + 1 + 2 = 10

Note that, for this challenge, we assume that the user will give a valid English word. We will not expect the computer to check that the word actually exists in the English language.

Web Address

http://www.101computing.net/scrabble-challenge/

Python Code

```
1.  #Scrabble Challenge - 101computing.net/scrabble-challenge
2.  from random import randint
3.
4.  #Using a dictionary we store the Scrabble value of each lett
    er of the alphabet
5.  letterValues= {"A":1,"B":3,"C":3,"D":2,"E":1,"F":4,"G":2,"H"
    :4,"I":1,"J":8,"K":5,"L":1,"M":3,"N":1,"O":1,"P":3,"Q":10,"R
    ":1,"S":1,"T":1,"U":1,"V":4,"W":4,"X":8,"Y":4,"Z":10}
```

```
6.
7.  #Let's generate 7 random letters and store them in a list ca
    lled letters
8.  randomLetters=[]
9.  for i in range(0,7):
10.     #Use ASCII code to generate  random letter between A (as
    cii code: 65) to Z (ascii code 90)
11.     randomLetter=chr(randint(65,90))
12.     randomLetters.append(randomLetter)
13.
14. print("###############################################")
15. print("#                                             #")
16. print("#              SCRABBLE CHALLENGE             #")
17. print("#                                             #")
18. print("###############################################")
19. print("\n")
20.
21. line1="" #will be used to display the 7 random letters
22. line2="" #will be used to display the value of each letter u
    nderneath
23.
24. for letter in randomLetters:
25.   line1 = line1 + "      " + letter
26.   line2 = line2 + "      " + str(letterValues[letter])
27.
28. print line1
29. print line2
30.
31. word=input("\nUse the given letters to create a word:").uppe
    r()
32. print("\nYour word: " + word)
33.
34. #Calculate the score of the word by adddding the score of eac
    h letter
35. score=0
36. for letter in word:
37.   score += letterValues[letter]
38.
39. #Check if the word is valid
40. valid=True
41. for letter in word:
42.   if letter not in randomLetters:
43.     valid=False
44.     score=0
45.   else:
46.     position = randomLetters.index(letter)
47.     del(randomLetters[position])
48.
49. #Output score or message to the use
```

```
50. if valid:
51.    print(score)
52. else:
53.    print("Invalid word!")
```

63. Hangman

For this challenge we are going to create a game of hangman. The computer will pick a word randomly within a given list of words. The player will have to guess the word by suggesting one letter at a time and the computer will automatically check if the letter given is included in the word to guess. If not, it will add one element to the hanged stick man drawing.

Web Address
http:// www.101computing.net/hangman-game/

Python Code

```
1.  #Hangman - www.101computing.net/hangman-game/
2.  import random
3.
4.  def drawHangman(life):
5.      if life==0:
6.          print ("                        ")
7.          print ("         _____         ")
8.          print ("        | /      |       ")
9.          print ("        |/     (~)       ")
10.         print ("        |       |        ")
11.         print ("        |    ---+---     ")
12.         print ("        |       |        ")
13.         print ("        |      / \      ")
14.         print ("        |     _/   \_ ")
15.         print ("        |                ")
16.         print ("       _|_               ")
17.         print ("                         ")
18.         print ("  ###############")
19.         print ("  #             #")
20.         print ("  #  GAME OVER  #")
21.         print ("  #             #")
22.         print ("  ###############")
```

143

```
23.     elif life==1:
24.         print ("                        ")
25.         print ("         _____       ")
26.         print ("        | /      |       ")
27.         print ("        |/    (~)        ")
28.         print ("        |      |         ")
29.         print ("        |   ---+---      ")
30.         print ("        |      |         ")
31.         print ("        |                ")
32.         print ("        |                ")
33.         print ("        |                ")
34.         print ("       _|_               ")
35.     elif life==2:
36.         print ("                        ")
37.         print ("         _____       ")
38.         print ("        | /      |       ")
39.         print ("        |/    (~)        ")
40.         print ("        |      |         ")
41.         print ("        |      |         ")
42.         print ("        |      |         ")
43.         print ("        |                ")
44.         print ("        |                ")
45.         print ("        |                ")
46.         print ("       _|_               ")
47.     elif life==3:
48.         print ("                        ")
49.         print ("         _____       ")
50.         print ("        | /      |       ")
51.         print ("        |/    (~)        ")
52.         print ("        |                ")
53.         print ("        |                ")
54.         print ("        |                ")
55.         print ("        |                ")
56.         print ("        |                ")
57.         print ("        |                ")
58.         print ("       _|_               ")
59.     elif life==4:
60.         print ("                        ")
61.         print ("         _____       ")
62.         print ("        | /      ")
63.         print ("        |/       ")
64.         print ("        |        ")
65.         print ("        |        ")
66.         print ("        |        ")
67.         print ("        |        ")
68.         print ("        |        ")
69.         print ("        |        ")
70.         print ("       _|_       ")
71.     elif life==5:
```

```
72.        print ("                    ")
73.        print ("          _         ")
74.        print ("          |         ")
75.        print ("          |         ")
76.        print ("          |         ")
77.        print ("          |         ")
78.        print ("          |         ")
79.        print ("          |         ")
80.        print ("          |         ")
81.        print ("          |         ")
82.        print ("         _|_        ")
83.    else:
84.        print ("                    ")
85.
86. #Initialise the game
87. listOfWords=["mouse","laptop","desktop","printer","keyboard"
    ]
88. wordToGuess=random.choice(listOfWords).upper()
89.
90. numberOfLives=6
91. wordSoFar=""
92. askedLetters = []
93.
94. for letter in wordToGuess:
95.    wordSoFar = wordSoFar + "_ "
96.
97. print(wordSoFar)
98.
99. #Start Playing
100.while (numberOfLives>0 and wordSoFar!=wordToGuess):
101.    print("\n")
102.    letter = input("What letter?").upper()
103.    askedLetters.append(letter)
104.
105.    if letter in wordToGuess:
106.        print("Good Guess")
107.        wordSoFar=""
108.        for character in wordToGuess:
109.            if character in askedLetters:
110.                wordSoFar = wordSoFar + character
111.            else:
112.                wordSoFar = wordSoFar + "_ "
113.        print(wordSoFar)
114.    else:
115.        print("You have lost a life")
116.        numberOfLives-=1
117.        drawHangman(numberOfLives)
118.
119.if numberOfLives>0:
```

145

```
120.   print("Well Done!")
121.else:
122.   print("Game Over!")
```

64. Roman Numerals Convertor

For this challenge we are writing a program used to convert whole numbers (integer) into roman numerals and vice versa.

Roman Numerals are based on seven symbols:

Symbol	Value
I	1
V	5
X	10
L	50

Symbol	Value
C	100
D	500
M	1,000

Web Address

http://www.101computing.net/roman-numerals-conversion/

Python Code

```
1.   #Roman Numerals Conversion - www.101computing.net/roman-
     numerals-conversion/
2.
3.   def integerToRoman(number):
4.     decimal = (1000,900,500,400,100,90,50,40,10,9,5,4,1)
5.     roman = ('M','CM','D','CD','C','XC','L','XL','X','IX','V',
       'IV','I')
6.     result = ""
7.     for i in range(0,len(decimal)):
8.       count = int(number / decimal[i])
9.       result += roman[i] * count
10.      number = number % decimal[i]
```

```
11.    return result
12.
13. def romanToInteger(romanNumber):
14.    romanNumber = romanNumber.upper()
15.    roman = ['M','D','C','L','X','V','I']
16.    decimal = [1000,500,100,50,10,5,1]
17.    places = []
18.    for i in range(0,len(romanNumber)):
19.      letter = romanNumber[i]
20.      #check if valid character
21.      if not letter in roman:
22.        return -1
23.      value = decimal[roman.index(letter)]
24.      # If the next place holds a larger number, this value is
     negative.
25.      if i<(len(romanNumber)-1):
26.        nextvalue = decimal[roman.index(romanNumber[i+1])]
27.        if nextvalue > value:
28.          value *= -1
29.      places.append(value)
30.    result = 0
31.    for number in places:
32.      result += number
33.    #Test if valid roman number format
34.    if integerToRoman(result) == romanNumber:
35.      return result
36.    else:
37.      return -1
38.
39. #Main Program Starts Here
40. print(" ---------- Roman Numberals Conversion ----------")
41. print(" > 1 - Convert an integer to a roman numerals,")
42. print(" > 2 - Convert a roman numerals to an interger.")
43. option=input("Choose an option (1 or 2):")
44. if option=="1":
45.    integer = int(input("Enter an integer (e.g. 2017):"))
46.    roman = integerToRoman(integer)
47.    print("Roman Numerals: " + roman)
48. elif option=="2":
49.    roman = input("Enter a roman numerals (e.g. MMXVII):")
50.    integer = romanToInteger(roman)
51.    print("Integer: " + str(integer))
52. else:
53.    print("invalid Option.")
```

65. Molecular Mass Calculator

The molecular weight (mass) of a molecule is calculated from the molecular formula of the substance; it is the sum of the atomic weights of the atoms making up the molecule. The molecular mass is expressed in atomic mass unit (amu).

For example, water has the molecular formula H_2O, indicating that there are two atoms of hydrogen and one atom of oxygen in a molecule of water.

Atom	Atomic Mass	Quantity	Total Mass (amu)
H	1.008	2	2.016
O	15.999	1	15.999
H_2O			18.015

For this challenge we will write a program that asks the end-user to enter a molecular formula of their choice. Using string manipulation techniques our Python script will break down the formula entered by the end-user and calculate the total mass of the molecule.

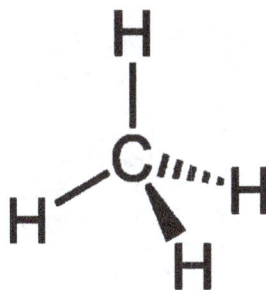

We will store the atomic mass of key atoms using a Python dictionary using the following data:

Atom	Atomic Mass (amu)
H	1.008
C	12.011
O	15.999
N	14.007

Atom	Atomic Mass (amu)
Fe	55.845
Ag	106.905
Cu	63.546
Na	22.989
Cl	35.453

To test your code, you can use the following molecules:

Molecule	Formula
Water	H_2O
Carbon Dioxide	CO_2
Methane	CH_4
Butane	C_4H_{10}
Carbonic Acid	H_2CO_3
Acetone	CH_3COCH_3
Lactose	$C_{12}H_{22}O_{11}$
Sodium Chloride	$NaCl$
Iron Oxide	Fe_2O_3
Copper Chloride Hydroxide	$HOCuCl$

Web Address

http://www.101computing.net/molecular-mass-calculator/

Python Code

```
1.  #Molecular Mass Calculator - www.101computing.net/molecular-
    mass-calculator/
2.
3.  #A Dictionary to store the atomic mass of the main atoms
4.  atomicMass = {"H":1.008, "O":15.999, "C":12.011, "N":14.007,
    "Fe":55.845, "Ag":106.905, "Cu": 63.546, "Na": 22.989,
    "Cl":35.453}
5.
6.  molecule = input("Please enter a molecule, e.g. H2O:")
7.  nextMass = 0
8.  massToUse = False
9.  totalMass = 0
10.
11. for j in range(0,len(molecule)):
12.   i = j
13.   number = ""
14.   isNumber = False
15.   #If not provided the number of atoms is 1
16.
17.   #The number of atoms could be more than one digit long: e.
      g. C12H22O11 will use 12 atoms of Carbon
18.   while molecule[i] in "1234567890":
```

```
19.      number = number + molecule[i]
20.      isNumber = True
21.
22.      i+=1
23.      if i>len(molecule)-1:
24.      break
25.
26.   if isNumber:
27.      if nextMass != 0:
28.       if massToUse:
29.        totalMass = float(totalMass)+(nextMass*int(number))

30.        massToUse = False
31.   if isNumber == False:
32.      #An atom start with an uppercase character, not a lowerc
    ase character
33.      if molecule[j] not in "abcdefghijklmnopqrstuvwxyz":
34.       if massToUse:
35.        totalMass = totalMass + nextMass
36.        massToUse = False
37.       #Some atoms however use two characters (Uppercase +low
    ercase characters) e.g. Fe or Cu
38.       if j+1<len(molecule):
39.        if molecule[j+1] in "abcdefghijklmnopqrstuvwxyz":
40.         nextMass = atomicMass[(molecule[j]+molecule[j+1])]

41.         massToUse = True
42.        else:
43.         nextMass = atomicMass[molecule[j]]
44.         massToUse = True
45.       else:
46.        nextMass = atomicMass[molecule[j]]
47.        massToUse = True
48.       massToUse = True
49.
50. if massToUse:
51.   totalMass = totalMass + float(nextMass)
52.
53. #Final Output
54. print("\nMolecule: " + molecule + " -
    Mass: " + str(totalMass) + " amu")
```

66. Caesar Cipher

In cryptography, a Caesar cipher, also known as shift cipher, is one of the simplest and most widely known encryption techniques. It is a type of substitution cipher in which each letter in the plaintext is replaced by a letter some fixed number of positions down the alphabet. For example, with a left shift of 3, D would be replaced by A, E would become B, and so on. The method is named after Julius Caesar, who used it in his private correspondence.

The action of a Caesar cipher is to replace each plaintext letter with a different one a fixed number of places down the alphabet.

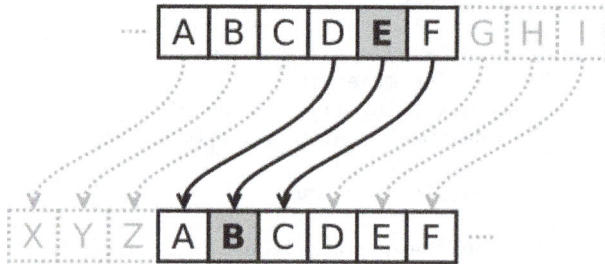

The cipher illustrated above uses a left shift of three, so that each occurrence of E in the plaintext becomes B in the ciphertext.

The transformation can be represented by aligning two alphabets; the cipher alphabet is the plain alphabet rotated left or right by some number of positions. For instance, here is a Caesar cipher using a left rotation of three places, equivalent to a right shift of 23 (the shift parameter is used as the key):

```
Plain:  ABCDEFGHIJKLMNOPQRSTUVWXYZ
Cipher: XYZABCDEFGHIJKLMNOPQRSTUVW
```

When encrypting, a person looks up each letter of the message in the "plain" line and writes down the corresponding letter in the "cipher" line.

```
Plaintext:   THE QUICK BROWN FOX JUMPS OVER THE
             LAZY DOG
Ciphertext:  QEB NRFZH YOLTK CLU GRJMP LSBO QEB
             IXWV ALD
```

Deciphering is done in reverse, with a right shift of 3.

The encryption can also be represented using modular arithmetic by first transforming the letters into numbers, according to the scheme, A = 0, B = 1,..., Z = 25. Encryption of a letter x by a shift n can be described mathematically as,

$$E_n(x) = (x + n) \mod 26.$$

Decryption is performed similarly,

$$D_n(x) = (x - n) \mod 26.$$

Did You Know?

The Caesar cipher is named after Julius Caesar, who used it, more than 2000 years ago, to protect messages of military significance.

Secret Message

In this challenge, our aim is to write a Python script to decode the following encrypted message, knowing that it has been encrypted using a right shift of 5 characters.

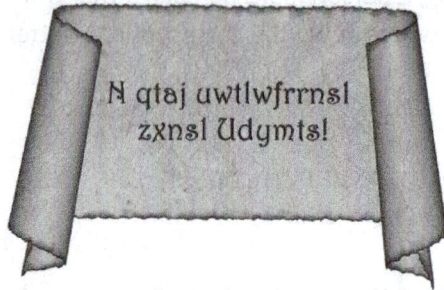

N qtaj uwtlwfrrnsl zxnsl Udymts!

N qtaj uwtlwfrrnsl zxnsl Udymts!
Key: right shift by 5 characters

Web Address

http://www.101computing.net/caesar-cipher/

Python Code

```
1.  #Caesar Cipher - www.101computing.net/caesar-cipher
2.  cipher = "N qtaj uwtlwfrrnsl zxnsl Udymts!"
3.  print("Cipher:")
4.  print(cipher)
5.  plainText = ""
6.  for character in cipher:
7.    ascii=ord(character)
8.    if ascii>=65 and ascii<=90: #UPPERCASE letter
9.      #Transpose index in the 0 o 25 range
10.     x = ascii - 65
11.     #Apply the decryption formula
12.     d = (x - 5) % 26
13.     #Transpose back to the 65 to 90 range
14.     ascii = d + 65
15.     plainText = plainText + chr(ascii)
16.   elif ascii>=97 and ascii<=122: #lowercase letter
17.     #Transpose index in the 0 o 25 range
18.     x = ascii - 97
19.     #Apply the decryption formula
20.     d = (x - 5) % 26
21.     #Transpose back to the 97 to 122 range
22.     ascii = d + 97
23.     plainText = plainText + chr(ascii)
24.   else: #Other character or punctuation sign
25.     plainText = plainText + character
26.
27. print("\nPlain Text:")
28. print(plainText)
```

Chapter #7: Date & Time Manipulation Techniques

When writing programs we sometimes have to manipulate **dates and times**. The operations we can do on these can be trickier than the usual arithmetic operations we have used so far. For instance we sometimes have to find the difference in days between two dates or add a specific amount of time to a date and time to find out what will be the resulting date and time.

Date and time information also needs to be formatted to be presented in a human readable format. To make things even more complex, not all countries use the same **date and time format**. For instance, while in the UK dates use the DD/MM/YYYY format, in the US they use the MM/DD/YYYY format!

The next few challenges will explore:

- Formatting Dates and Times,
- Performing Calculations based on Dates and Times.

DD/MM/YY

HH:MM:SS

The 12-hour clock is a time convention in which the 24 hours of the day are divided into two periods: a.m. (from the Latin ante meridiem, meaning "before midday") and p.m. (post meridiem, "after midday"). Each period consists of 12 hours numbered: 12 (acting as zero), 1, 2, 3, 4, 5, 6, 7, 8, 9, 10, and 11. The 24 hour/day cycle starts at 12 midnight (often indicated as 12 a.m.), runs through 12 noon (often indicated as 12 p.m.), and continues to the midnight at the end of the day.

This challenge consists of writing a computer program that asks the end-user to enter a time in the 24-hour format (e.g. 18:36). The program will convert this time in the 12-hour format (e.g. 6:36 PM).

Web Address

http://www.101computing.net/12-hour-clock/

Python Code

```
1.  #12 Hour Clock Time Convertor - www.101computing.net/12-
    hour-clock/
2.  #Input
3.  time=input("Enter a time in the hh:mm format (e.g 18:36)")
4.
5.  timeArray = time.split(":")
6.  hours = int(timeArray[0])
7.  minutes = int(timeArray[1])
8.
9.  #Process
10. ampm = ""
11. if hours == 12:
12.    ampm="PM"
13. elif hours == 0:
14.    ampm = "AM"
15.    hours=12
16. elif hours>=12:
17.    ampm="PM"
18.    hours = hours - 12
19. else:
20.    ampm="AM"
21.
```

```
22. #Output
23. print(str(hours) + ":" +str(minutes) + " " + ampm)
```

68. Marathon Time Calculator

In this challenge you are going to write a Python script to help a marathoner predict the overall time they can complete a Marathon in (42km).

This estimation will be based on the runner's pace which is the time they take to run 1km. For instance:

- Runner A runs 1km in 5:25 (5 minutes and 25 seconds)
- Runner B, who is slower, runs 1km in 6:10 (6 minutes and 10 seconds)

How long would runner A or runner B take to complete a full Marathon?

Web Address

http://www.101computing.net/marathon/

Python Code

```
1.  # Marathon Time Calculator - www.101computing.net/marathon
2.
3.  #String Manipulation Techniques...
4.  def left(string, numberOfCharacters):
5.      return string[:numberOfCharacters]
6.
7.  def right(string, numberOfCharacters):
8.      return string[-numberOfCharacters:]
9.
10. def locate(stringToFind, string):
11.     return string.find(stringToFind)
12.
13. print("Marathon Time Calculator")
14.
15. pace = input("At what pace do you run a km? e.g. 5:21")
16. split = locate(":",pace)
17. minutes = left(pace,split) #Retrieve the digits to the left
    of the ":"
```

```
18. seconds = right(pace,(len(pace)-split) - 1) # Retrieve the
    digits to the left of the ":
19.
20. kmtime = int(minutes)*60 + int(seconds) # e.g. 5:21 = 5 * 60
    + 21 = 321
21.
22. #42 km in a marathon
23. totaltime = 42 * kmtime  # e.g. 42 * 321 = 13482 seconds
24.
25. #Let's convert this into hh:mm:ss
26. hh = totaltime // 3600       # e.g. 13482 = 3 * 3600 +  2682
    (3 hours and 2682 seconds)
27. remainder = totaltime % 3600 # e.g. 2682
28. mm = remainder // 60 # e.g. 2682 = 44 * 60 + 42
29. ss = remainder % 60 # e.g. 42
30.
31. #Output
32. print("")
33. print("You will complete a marathon in " + str(hh) + ":" + s
    tr(mm) + ":" + str(ss))
```

69. Which Season?

Though we all agree that a calendar year is divided into four seasons, people sometimes disagree on the dates when these seasons start or finish. Many bodies, for example meteorologists, adopt a convention for the purpose of presenting statistics by grouping the twelve months of the year into four three-month seasons, for example March, April and May being taken as spring.

In this case the seasons could be defined as follows:

From	To	Season
1st September	30th November	Autumn
1st December	28/29th February	Winter
1st March	31st May	Spring
1st June	31st August	Summer

Other scientists and astronomers prefer to define the four seasons based on astronomical events known as the equinoxes and the solstices. The equinoxes occur in March and September when the Sun is 'edgewise' to the Earth's axis of rotation so that everywhere on Earth has twelve hours of daylight and twelve hours of darkness. The solstices occur in June and December when the Earth's axis is at its extreme tilt towards and away from the Sun so at mid-day it appears at its highest in one hemisphere and at its lowest in the other.

The exact dates for the solstices and equinoxes vary from one year to the other but are around the 21st of the months mentioned above.

For this challenge we will write a computer program that will retrieve today's date. The program will then display the season for this date based on the astronomical definition of the four seasons:

From	To	Season
21st September	20th December	Autumn
21st December	20th March	Winter
21st March	20th June	Spring
21st June	20th September	Summer

Web Address

http://www.101computing.net/which-season/

Python Code

```
1.  #Which Season? - www.101computing.net/which-season/
2.  from datetime import *
3.
4.  #Get Today's Date
5.  today = date.today()
6.  print("Today: " + today.strftime('%A %d, %b %Y'))
7.
8.  #Find out the starting dates of each season:
9.  thisYear = today.year
10. startOfSpring = date(thisYear,3,21) # March 21st
11. startOfSummer = date(thisYear,6,21) # June 21st
```

```
12. startOfAutumn = date(thisYear,9,21) # Sept 21st
13. startOfWinter = date(thisYear,12,21) # Dec 21st
14.
15. if today >= startOfSpring and today < startOfSummer:
16.    print("We are in Spring.")
17. elif today >= startOfSummer and today < startOfAutumn:
18.    print("We are in Summer.")
19. elif today >= startOfAutumn and today < startOfWinter:
20.    print("We are in Autumn.")
21. #Warning! Use an OR operator. This is because Winter is spli
    t (end and beginning of the calendar year!)
22. elif today >= startOfWinter or today < startOfSpring:
23.    print("We are in Winter.")
```

70. How Many Days Until Summer?

Summer starts on the Summer Solstice which, in the Northern hemisphere, is the 21st of June. It ends three months later, on September the 22nd, a date known as Autumnal equinox, when the autumn season starts.

For this challenge we will write a Python script that retrieves today's date to find out if we are in summer or not. If not, it will calculate the number of days until next summer; this could be in the same calendar year or in the following calendar year (in case we have already passed this year's summer season).

Web Address

http://www.101computing.net/days-until-summer/

Python Code

```
1. #Days left until Summer - www.101computing.net/days-until-
   summer/
2. from datetime import *
3.
4. #Get Today's Date
5. today = date.today()
6. print("Today: " + today.strftime('%d, %b %Y'))
7.
```

```
8.  #Find out the date of next summer:
9.  thisYear = today.year
10. startOfSummer = date(thisYear,6,21) # June 21st
11. endOfSummer = date(thisYear,9,22) # Sept. 22nd
12.
13. if today < startOfSummer:
14.   print("Next Summer: " + startOfSummer.strftime('%d, %b %Y
      '))
15.   #Calculate the number of days unitl next summer
16.   delta = (startOfSummer - today).days
17.   print(str(delta) + " days left until Summer!")
18. elif today >= startOfSummer and today <= endOfSummer:
19.   print("This is currently Summer!")
20. else:
21.   #We've passed this year's Summer, we will need to wait for
      next year!
22.   nextSummer = date(thisYear+1,6,21)
23.   print("Next Summer: " + nextSummer.strftime('%d, %b %Y'))

24.   delta = (nextSummer - today).days
25.   print(str(delta) + " days left until next Summer!")
```

71. How Old Will You Be In 2050?

For this challenge we will write a program to calculate how old we will be in 2050. The program will ask the user to enter their current age and calculate what their age will be in 2050.

Similar short challenges and solutions are also available at the web address provided below.

Web Address

http://www.101computing.net/year-2050/

Python Code

```
1. #How old will you be in 2050? - www.101computing.net/year-
   2050
2. from datetime import *
3.
```

```
4.  #Get Today's Date
5.  today = date.today()
6.  print("Today: " + today.strftime('%A %d, %b %Y'))
7.  thisYear = today.year
8.
9.  #Input user's age
10. age = int(input("How old are you?"))
11.
12. print("We are in " + str(thisYear) + " and you are " + str(a
    ge) + " years old.")
13.
14. #Calculating how old will the end-user be in 2050
15. print("In 2050 you will be...")
16. gap = 2050 - thisYear
17. print("..." + str(age+gap) + " years old!")
```

72. Happy Birthday!

For this challenge we are going to write a Python program that will ask the end-user to enter their date of birth in the following format: dd/mm/yyyy.

The program will then calculate and display the following information:
- The age of the user,
- The number of days the user has lived for,
- The week day (Monday to Sunday) corresponding to their date of birth,
- The number of days left until the user's next birthday,
- A "Happy Birthday" message if today is the user's birthday!

Web Address

http://www.101computing.net/happy-birthday/

Python Code

```
1.  #Happy Birthday - www.101computing.net/happy-birthday/
2.  from datetime import *
3.
4.  #Get Today's Date
5.  today = date.today()
```

```
6.  print("Today: " +  today.strftime('%A %d, %b %Y'))
7.
8.  dob_str = input("What is your Date of Birth? dd/mm/yyyy")
9.  #Convert user input into a date
10. dob_data = dob_str.split("/")
11. dob = date(int(dob_data[2]),int(dob_data[1]),int(dob_data[0]
    ))
12.
13. #Calculate number of days lived
14. numberOfDays = (today - dob).days
15.
16. #Convert this into whole years
17. age = numberOfDays // 365
18. print("You are " + str(age) + " years old.")
19.
20. #Retrieve the day of the week (Monday to Sunday) correspondi
    ng to the DoB.
21. day = dob.strftime("%A")
22. print("You were born on a " + day + ".")
23.
24. print("You have spent " + str(numberOfDays) + " days on Eart
    h.")
25.
26. #Calculating the number of days until next birthday
27. dobDay = dob.day
28. dobMonth = dob.month
29. thisYear = today.year
30.
31. nextBirthday = date(thisYear,dobMonth,dobDay)
32. if today<nextBirthday:
33.   gap = (nextBirthday - today).days
34.   print("Your birhday is in " + str(gap) + " days.")
35. elif  today == nextBirthday:
36.   print("Today is your birthday! Happy Birthday!")
37. else:
38.   nextBirthday = date(thisYear+1,dobMonth,dobDay)
39.   gap = (nextBirthday - today).days
40.   print("Your birthday is in " + str(gap) + " days.")
```

Chapter #8: File Handling Operations

Though variables and data structures such as lists and dictionaries are useful to temporary store values within our code, we sometimes need to access or save values into **external files**. This allows us to split the data from the actual code and to save data that will still be there even if the user quits the program. One approach to do this is to use a **text file**. The next few challenges will focus on:

- Reading, writing and appending data from/to a text file,
- Using CSV (Comma separated Values) files,
- Implementing a Linear Search and a Binary Search through a CSV file.

.TXT. .CSV

73. Random Name Picker

A school teacher sometimes asks questions to the whole class. They would like to have a program that helps them randomly pick a name from their class list.
They would like to make sure that once a name has been picked up once, they cannot be picked up a second time.

Using the class.txt file provided at the web address below, we will write a Python program to meet the teacher's requirements.

Web Address

http://www.101computing.net/team-generator/

Python Code

```
1.  #Random Name Picker - www.101computing.net/team-generator/
2.  from random import randint
3.
4.  #Step 1: Retrieve all pupils' names from text file
5.  file = open("class.txt","r")
6.  classList=[]
7.  for line in file:
8.      pupil = line.split(",")
9.      classList.append(pupil)
10. file.close()
11.
12. #Step 2: Random Name Picker
13. option=""
14. while len(classList)>0 and option<>"X":
15.     option = input("Press enter to pick a name or X to exit:")

16.     if option!="X":
17.         #Randomely pick a name form classList
18.         number = randint(0,len(classList)-1)
19.         print(">>>Name: " + classList[number][0] + " " + classLi
    st[number][1])
20.         #Remove name from classList so that they cannot be picke
    d again
21.         del(classList[number])
22.
23. print("The End.")
```

74. Team Generator

A school teacher has a class of 30 pupils stored in a text file called class.txt. This text file can be downloaded at the web address provided below.

The teacher would like to write a program that will help them make teams for group activities. The program will ask the number of teams the teacher needs (between 2 and 6), read the names of the pupils from the text file and assign pupils randomly to teams. The program will make sure that there is roughly (or exactly when possible) the same number of pupils in each team.

Web Address

http://www.101computing.net/team-generator/

Python Code

```
1.  #Team Generator - www.101computing.net/team-generator/
2.  from random import randint
3.
4.  numberOfTeams = int(input("How many teams would you like to
    create (between 1 and 6)?"))
5.  #Create a list of lists to store all the names in each team
6.  teams = []
7.  for team in range(0,numberOfTeams):
8.      teams.append([])
9.
10. #Step 1: Retrieve all pupils' names from text file
11. file = open("class.txt","r")
12. classList=[]
13. for line in file:
14.     pupil = line.split(",")
15.     classList.append(pupil)
16. file.close()
17.
18. #Step 2: Create teams
19. teamNumber=0
20. while len(classList)>0:
21.     #Randomely pick a name form classList
22.     number = randint(0,len(classList)-1)
23.
```

```
24.    #Append this pupil to a team
25.    teams[teamNumber].append(classList[number])
26.    teamNumber += 1
27.    if teamNumber == numberOfTeams:
28.      teamNumber = 0
29.
30.    #Remove name from classList so that they cannot be picked
   again
31.    del(classList[number])
32.
33. # Step 3: Display the composition of each team
34. for team in range(0,numberOfTeams):
35.   print("Team #" + str(team+1) + ":")
36.   for pupil in teams[team]:
37.     print("    " + pupil[0] + " " + pupil[1])
```

75. London 2012

In this challenge, we are going to investigate methods that can be used to:
- Read and extract data from a text file,
- Sort this data in ascending or descending order,
- Display this sorted data on screen.

You will find, at the web address provided below, a text file with the list of the ten top countries at the London 2012 Olympic Games. (Countries which won the most gold medals). This data is not sorted and is organised as follows:

Name of Country;Number of Gold Medals;Number of Silver Medals;Number of Bronze Medals

Our program will use this data to let the user sort the countries using five different options:
- In alphabetical (ascending) order of name of country,
- In descending order of gold medals,
- In descending order of silver medals,

- In descending order of bronze medals,
- In descending order of total number of medals (Bronze + Silver + Gold medals).

Web Address
http://www.101computing.net/london-2012/

Python Code

```
1.  #London Olympics 2012 - 101computing.net/london-2012/
2.
3.  ### Step 1 - open the text file
4.  file=open("countries.txt")
5.
6.  # Prepare the list (empty list to start with)
7.  countryList = []
8.
9.  # Read through the text file line by line
10. for eachLine in file:
11.     ### Step 2 - Extract the data from the text file
12.     splitData=eachLine.split(";")
13.     nameOfCountry = splitData[0]
14.     goldMedals = int(splitData[1])
15.     silverMedals = int(splitData[2])
16.     bronzeMedals = int(splitData[3])
17.     total = goldMedals + silverMedals + bronzeMedals
18.
19.     # Append this data to listOfCountries
20.     countryList.append([nameOfCountry, goldMedals, silverMed
    als, bronzeMedals, total])
21.
22. ### Step 3 – Sorting the list
23. print("Choose a sorting option:")
24. print("   1 -  Alphabetical Order")
25. print("   2 -  Descending order of Gold medals")
26. print("   3 -  Descending order of Silver medals")
27. print("   4 -  Descending order of Bronze medals")
28. print("   5 -  Descending order of total number of medals")
29. sortingOption = input("Type an option (1-5):")
30.
31. if sortingOption == "1":
32.   countryListSorted = sorted(countryList,key=lambda sort: so
    rt[0])
33. elif sortingOption == "2":
34.   countryListSorted = sorted(countryList,key=lambda sort: so
    rt[1], reverse=True)
```

```
35. elif sortingOption == "3":
36.    countryListSorted = sorted(countryList,key=lambda sort: so
       rt[2], reverse=True)
37. elif sortingOption == "4":
38.    countryListSorted = sorted(countryList,key=lambda sort: so
       rt[3], reverse=True)
39. elif sortingOption == "5":
40.    countryListSorted = sorted(countryList,key=lambda sort: so
       rt[4], reverse=True)
41.
42. ### Step 4 Loop through the sorted list and display each ent
    ry, one at a time.
43. print("\n######## London 2012 -
    Top 10 Countries ##########\n")
44. for eachCountry in countryListSorted:
45.    print(eachCountry[0] + " " + str(eachCountry[1]) + " gold
       medals + "
46.            + str(eachCountry[2]) + " silver medals + "
47.            + str(eachCountry[3]) + " bronze medals = "
48.            + str(eachCountry[4]) + " medals in total. ")
49.
50. ### Step 5 - Close the text file
51. file.close()
```

76. US Population - Statistics

For this challenge we will use the text file that you can download at the web address given below. This file contains a list of all 51 US states. The given text file is a CSV file (Comma Separated Values) with the following fields:

State , State Code , Population

Our aim is to write a Python program that will read through the data from the US States.txt text file to find out:

- The total population in the USA (by adding the population of each of the 51 states,
- The average population per state,
- The state which has the highest population,

- The state which has the lowest population,
- A list of all 51 states with their population as a percentage of the total US population.

Web Address

http://www.101computing.net/us-population/

Python Code

```
1.  #US Population Challenge - www.101computing.net/us-
    population/
2.
3.  #Open text file in read mode
4.  file = open("USStates.txt","r")
5.  min=999999
6.  max=0
7.  total=0
8.  count=0
9.  minState=""
10. maxState=""
11.
12. #Loop through the text file, line by line.
13. for line in file:
14.    stateFields = line.split(",")
15.    state=stateFields[0]
16.    code=stateFields[1]
17.    #For the last field we remove the last character (carriage
       return) and cast to an integer
18.    population=int(stateFields[2][:-1])
19.    if population<min:
20.      min=population
21.      minState=state
22.    if population>max:
23.      max=population
24.      maxState=state
25.    count+=1
26.    total+=population
27.    print(state + " (" + code + "): " + str(population))
28.
29. print("\n-------------------------")
30. print("State with the lowest Population:")
31. print(minState + " - " + str(min))
32. print("State with the highest Population:")
33. print(maxState + " - " + str(max))
34. print("Total US Population:")
35. print(total)
```

```
36. print("Average State Population:")
37. print(total//count)
38. print("-------------------------\n")
39.
40. #Displaying each state with its population as a percentage o
    f the total US population.
41. for line in file:
42.   stateFields = line.split(",")
43.   state=stateFields[0]
44.   code=stateFields[1]
45.   #For the last field we remove the last character (carriage
      return) and cast to an integer
46.   population=int(stateFields[2][:-1])
47.   print(state + " (" + code + "): " + str("%.2f" % ((populat
      ion/total)*100)) + "%")
48.
49. file.close()
```

77. US Population - Game

For this challenge we will use the text file that you can download at the web address given below. This file contains a list of all 51 US states with their name, two-letter code and their population.

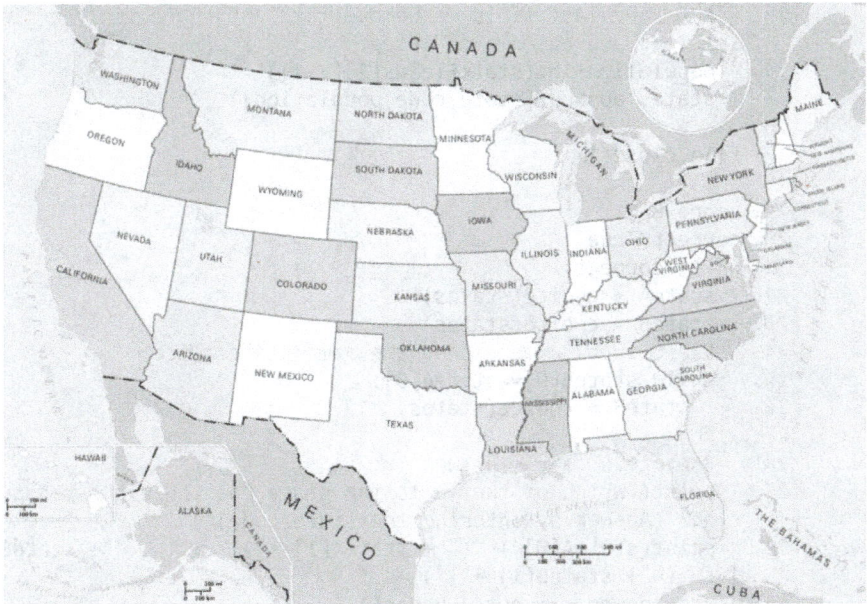

Using this text file we will create a Python game where the computer randomly displays two states on the screen (with their full name and their 2-letter code) and asks the user to guess which of the two states has the largest population. If the user guesses it right, they score one point otherwise they lose and the game ends.

Web Address

http://www.101computing.net/us-population/

Python Code

```
1.  #US Population Game - www.101computing.net/us-population/
2.  from random import choice
3.
4.  #Open text file in read mode
5.  file = open("USStates.txt","r")
6.  states=[]
7.
8.  #Loop through the text file, line by line.
9.  for line in file:
10.   stateFields = line.split(",")
11.   state=stateFields[0]
12.   code=stateFields[1]
```

```
13.    #For the last field we remove the last character (carriage
       return) and cast to an integer
14.    population=int(stateFields[2][:-1])
15.    states.append([state,code,population])
16.
17. file.close()
18.
19. score=0
20. correct=True
21. while correct:
22.    stateA = choice(states)
23.    stateB = choice(states)
24.    #Just in case we picked the same state twice
25.    while stateB[0]==stateA[0]:
26.      stateB = choice(states)
27.
28.    #Retrieve user's answer
29.    print("Which of the following state has the highest popula
       tion? (Answer by entering the state code)")
30.    print(stateA[0] + "(" + stateA[1] +")    vs.    " + stateB[0
       ] + "(" + stateB[1] +")")
31.    userAnswer = input().upper()
32.
33.    #Retrieve the state code of the state with the highest pop
       ulation
34.    if stateA[2]>stateB[2]:
35.      answer = stateA[1]
36.    else:
37.      answer = stateB[1]
38.
39.    #Did the user guess it right?
40.    if userAnswer==answer:
41.      score+=1
42.      print("Good guess - score: " + str(score) + "pts")
43.    else:
44.      print("Incorrect answer!")
45.      correct=False
46.
47. print("Game Over")
48. print("Final score: " + str(score) + "pts")
```

78. Google Translate

Have you ever used Google Translate to translate some text or a full webpage? For this challenge we are going to try to write a Python script to translate from English to French. However we are only going to translate numbers as follows:

Number	English	French
7	Seven	Sept
24	Twenty-four	Vingt-quatre
365	Three hundred and sixty-five	Trois cent soixante-cinq
25,642	Twenty-five thousand six hundred and forty-two	Vingt-cing mille six cent quarante-deux

From the examples given above, we can see that the same rules are used in both English and French to write numbers in full. This means that we can write a simple algorithm here to translate word for word each of the words used from English to French. Note that, even though this approach will be quite accurate to translate numbers written in full, it would be very inaccurate to translate full sentences. This is because the English grammar and the French grammar are different and though both languages have a lot of similarities, they do not follow exactly the same rules. (Grammar and conjugation)

For our translation algorithm we will focus on a word for word translation. To do so we need an English/French dictionary. We will use a text file containing all the words we need: One, Two, Three, ... Ten, Eleven, Twelve, ... Thirty, Forty, Fifty, ... Hundred, Thousand.

The text file can be downloaded at the web address provided below.

Python Code

```
1.  #French Translation Challenge - www.101computing.net/google-
    translate
2.
3.  print("Would you like to translate:")
4.  print(" 1 - From English to French?")
5.  print(" 2 - From French to English?")
6.  option = input("Type 1 or 2:")
7.
8.  if option=="1":
9.    myNumber = input("Type a number in English: e.g. Three hun
      dred and sixty-five")
10.   myNumber = myNumber.lower()
11.   print("\n>> Translating your number to French...\n")
12. else:
13.   myNumber = input("Type a number in French: e.g. Trois cent
      soixante-cinq")
14.   myNumber = myNumber.lower()
15.   print("\n>> Translating your number to English...\n")
16.
17. file = open("dictionary.txt", "r")
18.
19. for eachLine in file:
20.   words = eachLine.split(";")
21.   english = words[0]
22.   french = words[1]
23.   if option=="1":
24.     myNumber = myNumber.replace(english,french)
25.   else:
26.     myNumber = myNumber.replace(french,english)
27.
28. file.close()
29.
30. print(">> " + myNumber)
```

79. Class Register

This challenge consists of writing a Python program that could be used by a teacher to take the register at

the beginning of the lesson. By completing this challenge we will focus on accessing a text file in Python to:
- Read the content of the file line by line,
- Write data to a new file.

Our program will:
1. Read the text file called classList.txt, line by line.
2. For each student (line of the text file) the program should ask the teacher if the pupil is present ("/" code), absent for medical reasons or illness ("M" code), on a school trip ("T" code), or absent with no reason provided yet ("X" code).
3. The program should store the teacher's input alongside with the name of each pupil into a new text file called "register.txt".

To complete this challenge you will need to download and use the class list text file available at the web address provided below.

Web Address
http://www.101computing.net/class-register/

Python Code

```
1.  # Class Register Challenge - www.101computing.net/class-
    register/
2.
3.  print("####################")
4.  print("#                  #")
5.  print("#  Class Register   #")
6.  print("#                  #")
7.  print("####################")
8.  print("")
9.  print("Valid Codes:")
10. print("   /  - Present")
11. print("   M  - Medical Absence")
12. print("   T  - School Trip")
13. print("   A  - Authorised Absence")
14. print("   X  - No reason provided")
15. print("")
16. validCodes=["/","M","T","A","X"]
17.
18. #Open classList file in read mode
19. classList = open("classList.txt","r")
```

```
20.
21. #Open register file in (over)write mode
22. register = open("register.txt","w")
23.
24. for pupil in classList:
25.    fields = pupil.split(";")
26.    firstname = fields[0]
27.    lastname = fields[1]
28.    code = input(firstname + " " + lastname + "?")
29.    #Check if a valid code is entered
30.    while not code in validCodes:
31.        print("Invalid code - try again.")
32.        code = input(firstname + " " + lastname + "?")
33.
34.    #Store code with pupil's name
35.    register.write(code + " -
       " + firstname + " " + lastname + "\n")
36.
37. print(">>>The End.")
38.
39. #Close both files
40. classList.close()
41. register.close()
```

80. Le Tour De France

Le Tour de France is a cycling race that takes place over 21 stages (23 days in total, including two rest days). To complete this challenge you will need to download a text file available at the web address given below. This text file contains a list of the 21 stages as follows (based on the 2015 route):

Stage Number;Distance in km;Starting from;Arriving at

The aim of our program is to extract and analyse the data from this text file in order to answer the following questions:

- What stage is the longest stage (in distance)?
- What stage is the shortest stage (in distance)?
- What is the average distance per stage?

- What is the total distance of the race in miles?
- Between stage 16 and stage 17, once in Gap, cyclists have a rest day. How many kilometres have they been cycling for? How many kilometres are left till the end of the race?

Web Address
http://www.101computing.net/le-tour-de-france/

Python Code

```
1.  #Le Tour de France - www.101computing.net/tour-de-france/
2.
3.  file = open("letour.txt","r")
4.  totalDistance = 0
5.
6.  #Initialise Variables
7.  maxDistance=0
8.  maxStage=""
9.  minDistance=9999
10. minStage=""
11. numberOfStages=0
12. distanceUpToStage16 = 0
13.
14. #Let's loop through the text file one line (stage) at a time
    :
15. for stage in file:
16.   #Let's split the line into an array called "fields" using
      the ";" as a separator:
17.   fields =stage.split(";")
18.   currentStage = fields[0] + ": From: " + fields[2] + " To:
      " + fields[3] + " Distance: " + fields[1] + " km."
19.   print(currentStage)
20.   numberOfStages += 1
21.   stageDistance = float(fields[1])
22.   totalDistance += stageDistance
23.   if stageDistance > maxDistance:
24.     maxDistance = stageDistance
25.     maxStage = currentStage
26.   if stageDistance < minDistance:
27.     minDistance = stageDistance
28.     minStage = currentStage
29.   if numberOfStages < 17:
30.     distanceUpToStage16 += stageDistance
31.
32. print("_____")
33. print("Total Distance: " + str(totalDistance) + " km")
```

```
34.
35. print("_____")
36. print("Average Stage: " + str(round(totalDistance / numberOf
    Stages,1)) + " km")
37.
38. print("_____")
39. print("Longest Stage: " + maxStage)
40.
41. print("_____")
42. print("Shortest Stage: " + minStage)
43.
44. print("_____")
45. print("Distance from Stage 1 to Stage 16: " + str(distanceUp
    ToStage16) + " km")
46. print("Distance from Stage 17 till the end: " + str(totalDis
    tance - distanceUpToStage16) + " km")
47.
48. #It is good practice to close the file at the end to free up
    resources
49. file.close()
```

81. Secret Santa

This challenge consists of organising a Secret Santa list from a list of pupils. The program should output a list where each pupil is given the name of another pupil for who they need to get a present. For instance the output of the program may look like this:

- Laura will get a present for Ishaq,
- Ryan will get a present for Laura,
- Ishaq will get a present for Ryan.

With this challenge we will need to make sure that every pupil does receive a present and that a pupil does not end up having to give themselves a present.

Web Address

http://www.101computing.net/secret-santa/

```
1.  #Secret Santa - 101computing.net/secret-santa/
2.  from random import randint
3.
4.  groupList = ["Biba","Krystian","Karla","Thomas","Oliver","Ja
    mie","Satveer","Byron","Eldece","Kyle"]
5.
6.  index=randint(0,len(groupList)-1)
7.  startingName = groupList[index]
8.  #By removing the pupil from the list we make sure he/she wil
    l not be picked up twice.
9.  del groupList[index]
10.
11. nameFrom = startingName
12. for i in range(0,len(groupList)):
13.    index=randint(0,len(groupList)-1)
14.    nameTo = groupList[index]
15.    #By removing the pupil from the list we make sure he/she w
    ill not be picked up twice.
16.    del groupList[index]
17.    print(nameFrom + " will get a present for " + nameTo + ","
    )
18.    nameFrom=nameTo
19.
20. #Close the Loop: Last name to be picked up to get a present
    for the first name that has been picked
21. print(nameFrom + " will get a present for " + startingName +
    ".")
```

82. My Login Script

A lot of computer systems rely on the need for the user to login using a username and password. This form of authentication is used to uniquely identify a user and give them access to the relevant information on the system.

The aim of this challenge is to create our own authentication process. We will use a list of valid usernames and passwords stored in a text file called *usernames.txt*. This text file can be downloaded at the web address given below. It contains data organised in the following format:

Username;password;

Our challenge will allow the user to enter their username and password. It will then check if a user with the same username and password can be found in the text file (using a linear search).

The program will give up to three attempts for the user to get it right otherwise it will stop.

Web Address

http://www.101computing.net/my-login-script/

Python Code

```
1.  #My Login Script - www.101computing.net/my-login-script
2.  print("####################")
3.  print("#    Login Screen   #")
4.  print("####################")
5.
6.  #Opening the text file in read mode
7.  file = open("usernames.txt","r")
8.
9.  loggedIn = False
10. #Up to 3 attempts
11. for attempt in range(0,3):
12.    username = input("Username?")
13.    password = input("Password?")
14.
15.    #Linear Search through usernames.txt
16.    for line in file:
17.       data = line.split(",")
18.       if data[0]==username and data[1]==password:
19.          print("You are logged in.")
20.          loggedIn = True
21.          break
22.    if loggedIn == True:
23.       break
24.    else:
25.       print("Wrong username and password!")
26.
27. #Closing the text file
28. file.close()
```

83. CAPTCHA Challenge

A CAPTCHA is a type of challenge-response test used in computing to determine whether or not the user is human.

Web-bots are computer programs that can be used to try every single possible password to try to get access to a password protected system. We can stop web-bots by asking a question that web-bots may not understand. We will hence add a CAPTCHA to our login form (see previous challenge) to prevent web-bots trying to access our system.

Our CAPTCHA will be based on mathematical challenge: the computer will display a random arithmetic question such as "what is 7+3?". The user will have to answer this question correctly when login in.

Web Address

http://www.101computing.net/my-login-script/

Python Code

```
1.  #My Login Script - www.101computing.net/my-login-script
2.  import random
3.
4.  #A function to check if the user is human or not!
5.  def captcha():
6.    #Generate random arithmetic question
7.    operand1 = random.randint(0,10)
8.    operand2 = random.randint(0,10)
9.    operator = random.choice(["+","-","x"])
10.
11.   #Calculate expected answer
12.   correctAnswer = 0
13.   if operator == "+":
14.     correctAnswer = operand1+operand2
15.   elif operator == "-":
16.     correctAnswer = operand1-operand2
17.   elif operator == "x":
18.     correctAnswer = operand1*operand2
19.
20.   #Retrieve user answer
```

```
21.    userAnswer = input("What is " + str(operand1) + operator +
       str(operand2) + "?")
22.
23.    #Did the user get it right?
24.    if userAnswer==str(correctAnswer):
25.      return True
26.    else:
27.      return False
28.
29.
30. #Main Program Starts Here
31. print("####################")
32. print("#    Login Screen    #")
33. print("####################")
34.
35. #Opening the text file in read mode
36. file = open("usernames.txt","r")
37.
38. loggedIn = False
39. #Up to 3 attempts
40. for attempt in range(0,3):
41.    username = input("Username?")
42.    password = input("Password?")
43.    if captcha():
44.
45.      #Linear Search through usernames.txt
46.      for line in file:
47.        data = line.split(",")
48.        if data[0]==username and data[1]==password:
49.          print("You are logged in.")
50.          loggedIn = True
51.          break
52.      if loggedIn == True:
53.        break
54.      else:
55.        print("Wrong username and password!")
56.    else:
57.      print("Invalid CAPTCHA response.")
58.
59. #Closing the text file
60. file.close()
```

84. Where are you calling from?

This useful Python script will help you identify where
someone is calling you from based on their landline

phone number (UK only). It is based on a CSV file that contains all UK area codes and their corresponding location. The file is available at the web address given below. Our solution is based on a linear/serial search algorithm.

Web Address

http://www.101computing.net/where-are-you-calling-from/

Python Code

```
1.  #UK Phone Code Locator - www.101computing.net/where-are-you-
    calling-from/
2.  phoneNumber=input("Enter your phone number (UK landline only
    )")
3.  areaCode = phoneNumber[1:5]  #Extract the area code from the
    phone number
4.  print("Area Code: " + areaCode)
5.
6.  areaFound = False
7.  file = open("phonecodes.csv","r")
8.
9.  for line in file:   #Linear Search through the CSV file
10.   data = line.split(",")
11.   if data[0] == areaCode:
12.     print("You are calling from " + data[1])
13.     areaFound = True
14.     break
15.
16. if not areaFound:
17.   print("Sorry we cannot localise this number.")
18.
19. file.close()
```

85. UK Postcodes Distance Calculator

In this challenge, we will write a Python program that asks the end-user to enter two valid UK postcodes and in return displays the distance in miles or km between these two postcodes.

To complete this challenge we will first find the exact longitude and latitude of both the postcodes entered by the end-user. Our code will use a text file containing a list of all the UK outer codes (first part of a postcode) with their exact longitude and latitude. This file is available at the web address given below.

Once our program will have retrieved the longitude and latitude of both locations (postcodes) it will use the Haversine formula to calculate the exact distance between these two locations. The Haversine formula is an equation important in navigation, giving great-circle distances between two points on a sphere from their longitudes and latitudes. This formula will enable us to calculate the shortest distance over the earth's surface – giving an 'as-the-crow-flies' distance between the two locations (ignoring any hills they fly over, of course!).

Haversine Formula

$$a = \sin^2(\Delta\phi/2) + \cos\phi_1 \times \cos\phi_2 \times \sin^2(\Delta\lambda/2)$$

$$\textbf{distance} = 2 \times \text{Radius} \times \text{atan2}(\sqrt{a}, \sqrt{(1-a)})$$

ϕ is latitude, λ is longitude,
Radius *is the radius of the Earth (6,371km)*

Web Address
http://www.101computing.net/uk-postcode-distance-calculator/

Python Code

```
1.  #UK Postcodes Distance Calculator - www.101computing.net/uk-
    postcode-distance-calculator/
2.  import math
3.
4.  #postcode1=input("Enter a valid UK postcode:").upper()
5.  #postcode2=input("Enter a second UK postcode:").upper()
6.  postcode1="SW1A 1AA" #Buckingham Palace
7.  postcode2="EH1 1AA" #Edinburgh
8.
9.  #Extract outer codes
10. outerCode1=postcode1.split(" ")[0]
11. outerCode2=postcode2.split(" ")[0]
12.
13. latitude1=0
14. longitude1=0
15. latitude2=0
16. longitude2=0
17.
18. #Check files for postcodes (linear search) to retrieve corre
    sponding latitudes and longitudes from the text files
19. file = open("UKPostcodes.csv","r")
20. for line in file:
21.     fields = line.split(",")
22.     if len(fields)==4:
23.         if fields[1]==outerCode1:
24.             latitude1=fields[2]
25.             longitude1=fields[3]
26.         if fields[1]==outerCode2:
27.             latitude2=fields[2]
28.             longitude2=fields[3]
29.
30. print(postcode1)
31. print("Latitude 1: " + latitude1)
32. print("Longitude 1: " + longitude1)
33. print(postcode2)
34. print("Latitude 2: " + latitude2)
35. print("Longitude 2: " + longitude2)
36.
37. #Casting
38. latitude1=float(latitude1)
39. longitude1=float(longitude1)
40. latitude2=float(latitude2)
41. longitude2=float(longitude2)
42.
43. #Applying the Haversine formula
44. a = math.sin(math.radians((latitude1-
    latitude2)/2)) ** 2 + math.cos(math.radians(latitude1)) * ma
```

186

```
     th.cos(math.radians(latitude2)) * (math.sin(math.radians((lo
     ngitude1-longitude2)/2)) ** 2)
45.
46. Radius = 6371 #Earth Radius in km
47.
48. distance = 2 * Radius * math.atan2(math.sqrt(a),math.sqrt(1-
    a))
49. distance = math.trunc(distance)
50.
51. #Output results on screen
52. print("The distance between these two UK .based location is:\
    n")
53. print ("In km:")
54. print(str(distance) + " km\n")
55.
56. print ("In miles:")
57. distanceInMiles = math.trunc(distance/1.609)
58. print(str(distanceInMiles) + " miles")
```

Test Your Code and Compare Your Results

Use a website such as:

https://www.freemaptools.com/distance-between-uk-postcodes.htm

Compare the outputs or your program with the results given by this website which is using the same formula to calculate the distance "as the crow flies" between two UK postcodes.

86. Domain Name Server

Domain Name Servers (DNS) are the Internet's equivalent of a phone book. They maintain a directory of domain names and translate them to numerical IP addresses. These IP addresses are used to identify and locate the web-servers on the Internet network.

Domain names such *101computing.net* are easy for people to remember. Computers however access websites based on IP addresses, hence the

needs for domain name servers: when typing a website address in your web browser such as *http://www.101computing.net*, your request will reach a domain name server that will convert the domain name part of the address (*101computing.net*) into its matching IP address.

For this challenge we are going to create a Python script to "act as a domain name server". The script will ask the user to enter a domain name, search for this domain name within its own directory of domain names using a linear search and if found, return the matching IP address.

Our DNS script will use a text file with a short list of just 32 domain names and IP addresses. This data is organised as follows:

Domain Name,IP Address

You can download this CSV file at the web address provided below.

Web Address

http://www.101computing.net/domain-name-server/

Method #1: Using a Linear Search

To find the requested domain name we will first implement a linear search: Our algorithm will read the *dns.csv* file one line at a time and check if the domain name is a match.

Below is the flowchart of a linear search:

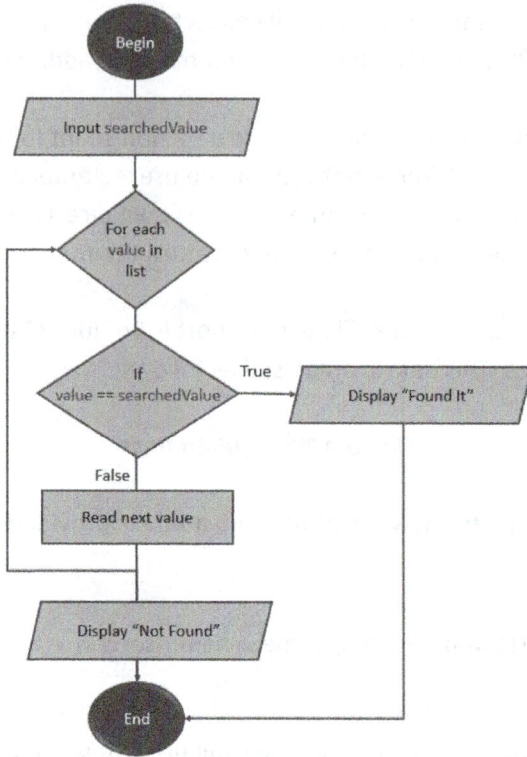

Linear / Serial Search

Python Code: Method #1: Using a Linear Search

```
1.  #Domain Name Server Script - www.101computing.net/domain-
    name-server/
2.  domainName = input("Enter a domain name: (e.g. google.com)")

3.
4.  #Open csv file in read mode
5.  file = open("dns.csv","r")
6.  domainFound = False
7.
8.  #Perform a linear search to find and output the matching IP
    address
9.  for line in file:
10.   data = line.split(",")
11.   if data[0]==domainName:
12.     print("Domain found:")
13.     print("IP Address: " + data[1])
```

```
14.        domainFound = True
15.        #Exit loop
16.        break
17.
18. if not domainFound:
19.    print("Cannot find this domain name.")
20.
21. #Close the csv file
22. file.close()
```

Method #2: Using a Binary Search

You may have noticed that the list of domain names in the *dns.csv* file is sorted in alphabetical order. This is a key requirement to implement a binary search, a more efficient approach to search through a sorted set of data.

Below is the flowchart of a binary search:

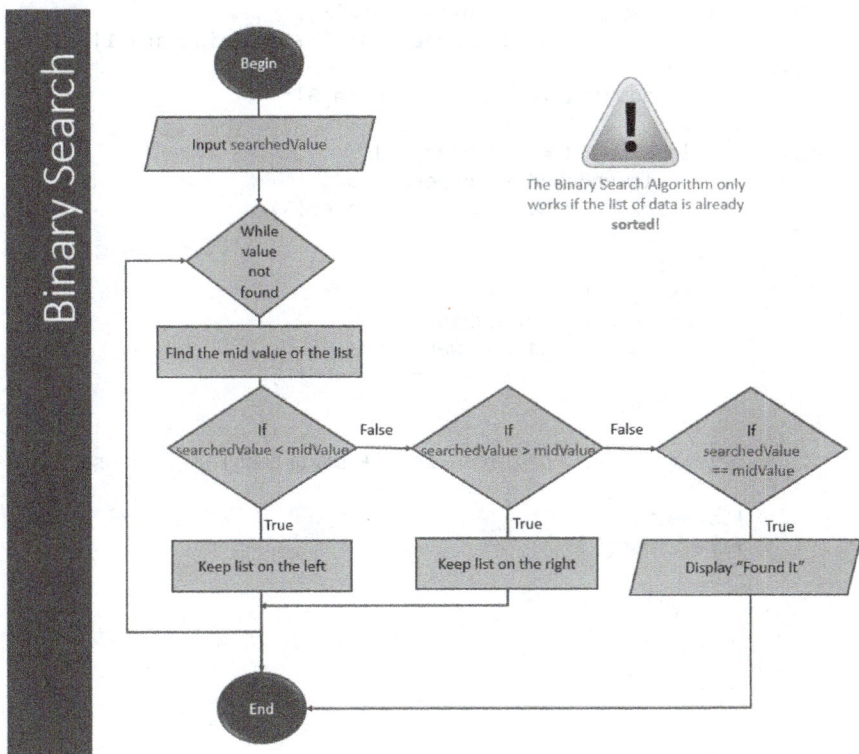

The Binary Search Algorithm only works if the list of data is already **sorted!**

```
1.  #Domain Name Server Script - www.101computing.net/domain-
    name-server/
2.  domainName = input("Enter a domain name: (e.g. google.com)")

3.
4.  #Open csv file in read mode
5.  file = open("dns.csv","r")
6.  lines = file.readlines()
7.
8.  #Perform a binary search to find and output the matching IP
    address
9.  lowerBound = 0
10. upperBound = len(lines)
11. steps = 0
12.
13. while True:
14.    steps += 1
15.    midPoint = (lowerBound + upperBound) // 2
16.    midPointData = lines[midPoint].split(",")
17.
18.    if domainName == midPointData[0]:
19.       print("Matching IP address: " + midPointData[1])
20.       break
21.    elif domainName > midPointData[0]:
22.       #Keep list on the right
23.       lowerBound = midPoint + 1
24.       if lowerBound >= upperBound:
25.          print("Domain name not found!")
26.          break
27.    else:
28.       #Keep list on the left
29.       upperBound = midPoint - 1
30.       if upperBound < lowerBound:
31.          print("Domain name not found!")
32.          break
33.
34. print("Search completed in " + str(steps) + " steps.")
35.
36. #Close the csv file
37. file.close()
```

Chapter #9: 2D and 3D Representation

Most of our challenges so far have been based on a text-based interface. A this stage you are most likely longing to create your own programs or video games based on a Graphical User Interface. Before doing so though we recommend you to gain a very good understanding of how **(x,y) and (x,y,z) coordinates** can be used within a Python program to draw 2D or 3D shapes on the screen. The following challenges will help you investigate the following concepts:

- Python Turtle,
- (x,y) Coordinates,
- (x,y,z) Coordinates.

Challenges 87 - 97 are based on the **Python Turtle library**, included per default in the Python package.

Challenges 98 – 99 are based on **GlowScript and VPython**. GlowScript is an easy-to-use, powerful environment for creating 3D animations and publishing them on the web. VPython, a language based on the Python syntax, lets you write and run programs in the GlowScript environment

Find out more about GlowScript and VPython:
http://www.glowscript.org/docs/VPythonDocs/index.html

Challenge 100 is based on the **Processing library** which enables to work on 2D/3D projects with Python. You can find out more about the Processing library for Python on:
http://py.processing.org/

Our challenge is to guide the turtle through a maze (See picture below). To do so we will need to use the following instructions:

- *myPen.forward(100)* to move forward by 100 pixels,
- *myPen.right(90)* to turn right by 90 degrees,
- *myPen.left(90)* to turn left by 90 degrees.

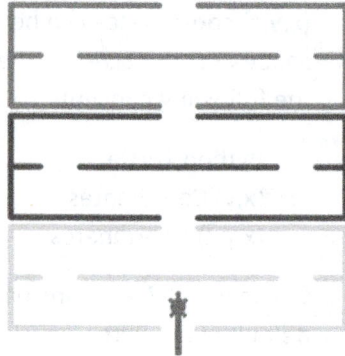

To minimise the number of lines of code we will use a *for loop* to repeat a set of instructions three times, for each of the three layers of this maze.

Web Address

http://www.101computing.net/turtle-maze/

Python Code

```
1.  #Turtle Maze Challenge - www.101computing.net/turtle-maze/
2.  import turtle
3.  import maze
4.
5.  myPen=turtle.Turtle()
6.  myPen.penup()
7.  myPen.goto(20,-180)
8.  myPen.pendown()
9.  myPen.shape('turtle')
10. myPen.color("#DB148E")
11. myPen.width(5)
12. myPen.left(90)
13.
14. #Start of maze
15. myPen.forward(70)
16.
17. for i in range(0,3):
18.    myPen.right(90)
```

```
19.    myPen.forward(120)
20.    myPen.left(90)
21.    myPen.forward(50)
22.    myPen.left(90)
23.    myPen.forward(120)
24.    myPen.right(90)
25.    myPen.forward(60)
```

88. Snowflake Challenge

In this challenge, we will use our Python Turtle skills to draw a snowflake. We will first draw the first branch of the snowflake as follows:

Then will use iteration (For Loop) to recreate each branch of the snowflake.

Web Address

http://www.101computing.net/snowflake-challenge/

Python Code

```
1.    #Snowflake Challenge - www.101computing.net/snowflake-
      challenge/
2.    import turtle
3.
4.    myPen = turtle.Turtle()
5.    myPen.shape("heart")
6.    myPen.speed(500)
```

```
7.
8.  mypen.color("#3333FF")
9.
10. mypen.left(90)
11. #Use a for loop to repeat the branch pattern 6 times
12. for i in range (1,7):
13.     mypen.forward(100)
14.     mypen.forward(-30)
15.     mypen.left(60)
16.     mypen.forward(30)
17.     mypen.forward(-30)
18.
19.     mypen.right(120)
20.     mypen.forward(30)
21.     mypen.forward(-30)
22.
23.     mypen.left(60)
24.     mypen.forward(-70)
25.     mypen.left(60)
```

89. Astronomy Challenge

In astronomy, a constellation is a grouping of stars on the celestial sphere perceived as a figure or design. There are 88 recognized constellations and each of these have been named after characters from classical Greek and Roman mythology as well as various common animals and objects.

In this challenge we are using Python Turtle to draw famous constellations on the screen.

Each constellation is saved as a list. Each value of the list represents a star. Each star is also a list with only 2 values, the x and y coordinates of the star (drawn on a 2D screen). So a constellation is stored as a list of lists!

For instance, for Cassiopeia:
cassiopeia = [[-90,70],[-50,-10],[0,0],[40,-50],[100,0]]

195

Using a for loop we can then read the content of the constellation, to plot each star on the screen, one at a time, based on its x and y coordinates.

The Plough

Leo

Cassiopeia

Web Address
http://www.101computing.net/astronomy-challenge/

Python Code

```
1.  #Astronomy Challenge - www.101computing.net/constellations
2.  import turtle
3.
4.  #Initialise Pythn Turtle and Screen
5.  myPen = turtle.Turtle()
6.  myPen.speed(0)
7.  window = turtle.Screen()
8.  window.bgcolor("#000088")
9.  myPen.color("#FFFFFF")
10.
11. def drawConstellation(constellation):
12.    #draw the first star
13.    myPen.penup()
14.    myPen.goto(constellation[0])
15.    myPen.begin_fill()
16.    myPen.circle(2)
17.    myPen.end_fill()
18.    myPen.pendown()
19.    #draw each line and star within the constellation
20.    for star in constellation:
21.       myPen.goto(star)
22.       myPen.begin_fill()
23.       myPen.circle(2)
24.       myPen.end_fill()
25.    #hide the turtle
26.    myPen.penup()
```

196

```
27.    myPen.goto(600,600)
28.
29. #Define Constellations as a list of (x,y) coordinates
30. plough = [[-140,20],[-60,25],[0,10],[35,-5],[45,-50],[120,-
    60],[150,-5]]
31. cassiopeia = [[-90,70],[-50,-10],[0,0],[40,-50],[100,0]]
32. leo = [[10,30],[50,10],[60,-40],[-90,-50],[-180,-70],[-
    110,0],[10,30],[15,80],[60,130],[80,120]]
33. lyra = [[30,75],[-60,73],[-150,1-100],[-50,-
    110],[30,75],[50,120],[80,90],[30,75]]
34.
35. #drawConstellation(plough)
36. #drawConstellation(cassiopeia)
37. #drawConstellation(leo)
38. drawConstellation(lyra)
```

90. Python Turtle Clock

This challenge consists of using the Python turtle library and the datetime library to create a program that displays the current time as an anlogue clock.

The first part of the program will display the clock with all the graduations. The second part of the program will draw the three handles (hours, minutes, seconds). To complete this challenge we need to do some angle calculations to understand what angles to use when displaying the small hand (hours) and the big hand (minutes). We invite you to find out more about these calculations by reading the blog post at the web address given below.

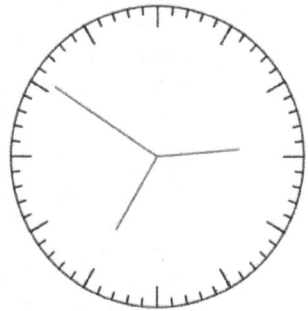

Web Address

http://www.101computing.net/python-turtle-clock/

```
1.  #Python Turtle Clock - www.101computing.net/python-turtle-
    clock/
2.  from datetime import datetime
3.  import turtle
4.
5.  myPen = turtle.Turtle()
6.  myPen.tracer(0)
7.  myPen.speed(0)
8.  myPen.hideturtle()
9.
10. currentMinute = datetime.datetime.now().minute
11. currentHour = datetime.datetime.now().hour
12. currentSecond = datetime.datetime.now().second
13.
14. #Draw Circle
15. myPen.penup()
16. myPen.goto(0,-180)
17. myPen.pendown()
18. myPen.color("blue")
19. myPen.circle(180)
20.
21. #Draw 12 Graduations (Hours)
22. for i in range(0,12):
23.     myPen.penup()
24.     myPen.goto(0,0)
25.     #Point to the top - 12 o'clock
26.     myPen.setheading(90)
27.     myPen.right(i*360/12)
28.     myPen.forward(155)
29.     myPen.pendown()
30.     myPen.forward(25)
31.
32. #Draw 60 Graduations (Minutes)
33. for i in range(0,60):
34.     myPen.penup()
35.     myPen.goto(0,0)
36.     #Point to the top - 12 o'clock
37.     myPen.setheading(90)
38.     myPen.right(i*360/60)
39.     myPen.forward(170)
40.     myPen.pendown()
41.     myPen.forward(10)
42.
43. myPen.color("red")
44. #Calculate angle and draw hour hand
45. myPen.penup()
46. myPen.goto(0,0)
```

```
47. myPen.setheading(90) # Point to the top - 12 o'clock
48. myPen.right(currentHour*360/12 + (currentMinute * 0.5))
49. myPen.pendown()
50. myPen.forward(100)
51.
52. #Calculate angle and draw minute hand
53. myPen.penup()
54. myPen.goto(0,0)
55. myPen.setheading(90) # Point to the top - 0 minute
56. myPen.right((currentMinute*360/60) + (currentSecond/10))
57. myPen.pendown()
58. myPen.forward(150)
59.
60. myPen.color("green")
61. #Calculate angle and draw second hand
62. myPen.penup()
63. myPen.goto(0,0)
64. myPen.setheading(90) # Point to the top - 0 second
65. myPen.right(currentSecond*360/60)
66. myPen.pendown()
67. myPen.forward(100)
68.
69. myPen.getscreen().update()
```

91. Python Turtle Challenge

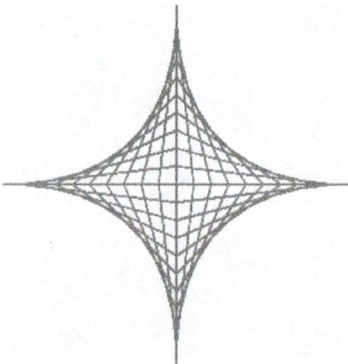

In this challenge, we are going to use the turtle library to draw this complex shape.

To understand the code of this challenge, you will need a good understanding of how (x,y) coordinates work.

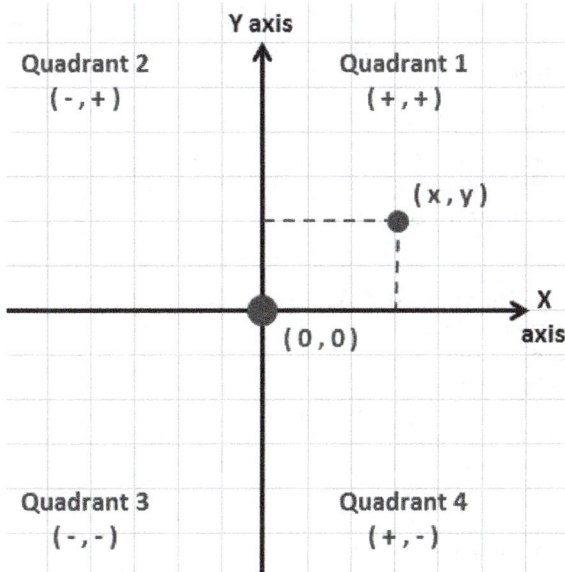

http://www.101computing.net/python-turtle-challenge/

Python Code

```
1.  #Python Turtle - http://www.101computing.net/python-turtle-
    challenge/
2.  import turtle
3.
4.  #Initialise the turtle
5.  myPen = turtle.Turtle()
6.  myPen.shape("arrow")
7.  myPen.color("red")
8.  myPen.delay(1)
9.  myPen.hideturtle()
10.
11. # (+,+) quadrant
12. for i in range(0,11):
13.    yFrom=10-i
14.    xTo=i
15.    myPen.penup()
16.    myPen.goto(0,20*yFrom)
```

```
17.    myPen.pendown()
18.    myPen.goto(20*xTo,0)
19.
20. # (-,+) quadrant
21. for i in range(0,11):
22.    yFrom=10-i
23.    xTo=-i
24.    myPen.penup()
25.    myPen.goto(0,20*yFrom)
26.    myPen.pendown()
27.    myPen.goto(20*xTo,0)
28.
29. # (+,-) quadrant
30. for i in range(0,11):
31.    yFrom=-10+i
32.    xTo=i
33.    myPen.penup()
34.    myPen.goto(0,20*yFrom)
35.    myPen.pendown()
36.    myPen.goto(20*xTo,0)
37.
38. # (-,-) quadrant
39. for i in range(0,11):
40.    yFrom=-10+i
41.    xTo=-i
42.    myPen.penup()
43.    myPen.goto(0,20*yFrom)
44.    myPen.pendown()
45.    myPen.goto(20*xTo,0)
```

92. Archery Scoring Algorithm

For this challenge, we will write a Python program to randomly shoot an arrow on a target. We will then use Pythagoras' Theorem to calculate the distance between the arrow impact and the centre of the target. This distance will let us find out how many points to award to this shoot.

We will shoot three arrows and calculate and display the cumulative score of these three arrows.

Scoring System:

For our program we will be using the following scoring system:

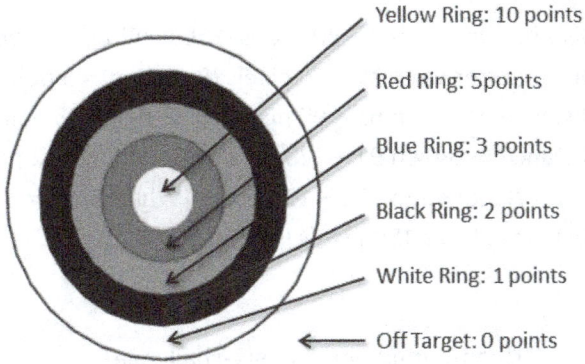

Yellow Ring: 10 points

Red Ring: 5points

Blue Ring: 3 points

Black Ring: 2 points

White Ring: 1 points

Off Target: 0 points

Pythagoras' Theorem:

The arrow will be issued (x,y) coordinates randomly. Our script will use these coordinates to calculate the distance of the arrow from the centre of the target (0,0).

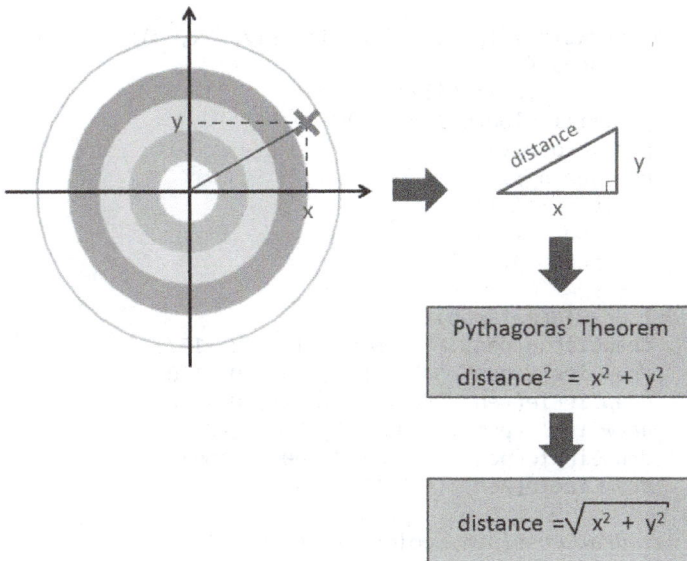

Pythagoras' Theorem

$$distance^2 = x^2 + y^2$$

$$distance = \sqrt{x^2 + y^2}$$

With this distance, we can then decide how many points to be given using the following criteria:

- Distance between 0 – 30 pixels (Yellow Ring) = 10 points
- Distance between 31 – 60 pixels (Red Ring) = 5 points
- Distance between 61 – 90 pixels (Blue Ring) = 3 points
- Distance between 91 – 120 pixels (Black Ring) = 2 points
- Distance between 121 – 150 pixels (White Ring) = 1 point
- Distance above 150 pixels (Off Target) = 0 point

Web Address

http://www.101computing.net/archery-challenge/

Python Code

```
1.  #Archery Challenge - www.101computing.net/archery-
    challenge
2.
3.  import turtle
4.  import random
5.  import time
6.
7.  def drawCircle(pen, colorFill, size, x, y):
8.      pen.penup()
9.      pen.color(colorFill)
10.     pen.fillcolor(colorFill)
11.     pen.goto(x,y)
12.     pen.begin_fill()
13.     pen.circle(size)
14.     pen.end_fill()
15.     pen.pendown()
16.
17. def drawTarget(pen):
18.     drawCircle(pen, "#000000", 152, 0,-152)
19.     drawCircle(pen, "#FFFFFF", 150, 0,-150)
20.     drawCircle(pen, "#000000", 120, 0,-120)
21.     drawCircle(pen, "#33AAFF", 90, 0,-90)
22.     drawCircle(pen, "#FF0000", 60, 0,-60)
23.     drawCircle(pen, "#FFFF00", 30, 0,-30)
24.
25. def drawCross(pen, color, size, x, y):
26.     pen.pensize(3)
27.     pen.color(color)
28.     pen.penup()
```

```
29.    pen.goto(x-size,y-size)
30.    pen.pendown()
31.    pen.goto(x+size,y+size)
32.    pen.penup()
33.    pen.goto(x-size,y+size)
34.    pen.pendown()
35.    pen.goto(x+size,y-size)
36.
37. def writeScore(pen, text):
38.    pen.penup()
39.    pen.goto(-80, 170)
40.    pen.color("#000000")
41.    pen.write(text, None, None, "16pt bold")
42.
43. def calculateScore(arrowx,arrowy):
44.    import math
45.    score = 0
46.    distance = math.sqrt((arrowx ** 2) + (arrowy ** 2))
47.    if distance <= 30 :
48.       #distance between 0 - 30 (Yellow) = 10 points
49.       score = score + 10
50.    elif distance > 30 and distance <= 60 :
51.       #distance between 31 - 60 (Red) = 5 points
52.       score = score + 5
53.    elif distance > 60 and distance<= 90 :
54.       #distance between 61 - 90 (Blue) = 3 points
55.       score = score + 3
56.    elif distance > 90 and distance<= 120 :
57.       #distance between 91 - 120 (Black) = 2 points
58.       score = score + 2
59.    elif distance > 120 and distance <= 150 :
60.       #distance between 121 - 150 (White) = 1 point
61.       score = score + 1
62.
63.    return score
64.
65.
66. #Main Program Starts Here
67. myPen = turtle.Turtle()
68. myPen.tracer(0)
69. myPen.speed(0)
70. myPen.hideturtle()
71. myPen.shape("arrow")
72. score=0
73. drawTarget(myPen)
74.
75. #Shoot 3 arrows
76. for i in range (0,3):
77.    time.sleep(1)
```

```
78.   #Shooting the arrow
79.   arrowx= random.randint(-150,150)
80.   arrowy= random.randint(-150,150)
81.   drawCross(myPen,"#FF7777",10,arrowx,arrowy)
82.   score += calculateScore(arrowx,arrowy)
83.   myPen.penup()
84.   myPen.getscreen().update()
85.
86. #Display score
87. writeScore(myPen,"Your Score:  " + str(score))
88.
89. myPen.getscreen().update()
```

93. Randomised Christmas Cards

For this challenge we are going to create a Christmas card using Python turtle. We will use the random library to create unique cards.

You can access some already coded cards at the web address provided below.

This challenge provides a great opportunity to develop your understanding of (x,y) coordinates and of how these can be used to draw and position various shapes on screen.

The code provided below is used to create the "random forest" card (see picture above) using a range of Christmas trees of random size, colours and position on the card as well as random snowflakes.

http://www.101computing.net/chirstmas-tree/

```
1.  # Christmas Tree Challenge - www.101computing.net/christmas-
    tree/
2.  import turtle
3.  import random
4.
5.  #3 Functions to draw various shapes on screen
6.  def draw_circle(turtle, color, x, y, radius):
7.      turtle.penup()
8.      turtle.color(color)
9.      turtle.fillcolor(color)
10.     turtle.goto(x,y)
11.     turtle.pendown()
12.     turtle.begin_fill()
13.     turtle.circle(radius)
14.     turtle.end_fill()
15.
16. def draw_triangle(turtle, color, x, y, width, height):
17.     turtle.penup()
18.     turtle.color(color)
19.     turtle.fillcolor(color)
20.     turtle.goto(x,y)
21.     turtle.pendown()
22.     turtle.begin_fill()
23.     turtle.goto(x+width,y)
24.     turtle.goto(x+width/2,y+height)
25.     turtle.goto(x,y)
26.     turtle.end_fill()
27.     turtle.setheading(0)
28.
29. def draw_rectangle(turtle, color, x, y, width, height):
30.     turtle.penup()
31.     turtle.color(color)
32.     turtle.fillcolor(color)
33.     turtle.goto(x,y)
34.     turtle.pendown()
35.     turtle.begin_fill()
36.     for i in range (2):
37.         turtle.forward(width)
38.         turtle.left(90)
39.         turtle.forward(height)
40.         turtle.left(90)
41.     turtle.end_fill()
42.     turtle.setheading(0)
```

206

```
43.
44. myPen = turtle.Turtle()
45. myPen.shape("turtle")
46. myPen.speed(10)
47. window = turtle.Screen()
48. window.bgcolor("#FFFFFF")
49. draw_circle(myPen, "#69D9FF", 0, -200, 200)
50.
51. #Snow - 15 Snowflakes
52. for i in range (1,16):
53.    x = random.randint(-180,200)
54.    y = random.randint(-120, 180)
55.    size = random.randint(5,10)
56.    draw_circle(myPen, "white", x, y, size)
57.
58. #Trees - 7 trees of different sizes and green colours
59. greens = ["#017711","#2ABF3D","#387C44", "#347C17"]
60. for i in range (1,8):
61.    x = random.randint(-120,120)
62.    y = -80
63.    width = random.randint(5,15)
64.    height = random.randint(20,30)
65.    draw_rectangle(myPen, "#7F462C", x, y, width, height)
66.    tr_width = random.randint(40,120)
67.    tr_height = random.randint(60,180)
68.    color = random.choice(greens)
69.    draw_triangle(myPen, color, x-
       tr_width/2+width/2, y+height, tr_width, tr_height)
70.
71. #Card Message
72. myPen.penup()
73. myPen.color("red")
74. myPen.goto(-100, -150)
75. myPen.write("Merry Christmas", None, None, "24pt bold",)
76. myPen.hideturtle()
```

94. Gradient Animation

In this challenge we are going to create some animated gradients by progressively changing the colour of the screen from one colour (e.g. green) to another (e.g. yellow).

RGB Colour Codes:
Did you know that every colour on the screen can be represented using an RGB code (Red, Green, Blue). This code consists of three numbers between 0 and 255, indicating how much red, green and blue are used to recreate the colour.

For instance the RGB code for:
- Red is (255,0,0)
- Green is (0,255,0)
- Blue is (0,0,255)
- Yellow is (255,255,0)
- Orange is (255,165,0)

The web address given below lists some of the gradients you will need to recreate. The solution given below focuses on Gradient #5: from green (0,255,0) to yellow (255,255,0) to magenta (255,0,255) to cyan (0,255,255) to green (0,255,0).

Web Address
http://www.101computing.net/gradient-animation/

```
1.  #Gradient Animation - www.101computing.net/gradient-
    animation
2.
3.  import turtle
4.  import time
5.  window = turtle.Screen()
6.
7.  #Repeat the pattern 3 times
8.  for count in range(0,3):
9.    #From green (0,255,0) to yellow (255,255,0)
10.   for i in range(0,255):
11.     red = i
12.     green = 255
13.     blue = 0
14.     window.bgcolor(red,green,blue)
15.     time.sleep(0.001)
16.
17.   #From yellow (255,255,0) to magenta (255,0,255)
18.   for i in range(0,255):
19.     red = 255
20.     green = 255 - i
21.     blue = i
22.     window.bgcolor(red,green,blue)
23.     time.sleep(0.001)
24.
25.   #From magenta (255,0,255) to cyan (0,255,255)
26.   for i in range(0,255):
27.     red = 255 - i
28.     green = i
29.     blue = 255
30.     window.bgcolor(red,green,blue)
31.     time.sleep(0.001)
32.
33.   #From cyan (0,255,255) to green (0,255,0)
34.   for i in range(0,255):
35.     red = 0
36.     green = 255
37.     blue = 255 - i
38.     window.bgcolor(red,green,blue)
39.     time.sleep(0.001)
```

95. Gradient Generator

This challenge consists of creating a palette of eight colours using a gradient effect. The user will be prompted to enter two colours (using the RGB colour code) and our program will automatically calculate six RGB colour codes to create a linear gradient between both given colours.

Using Python Turtle we will then represent this colour palette on the screen as follows:

Web Address

http://www.101computing.net/gradient-generator/

Python Code

```
1.  #Gradient Generator - www.101computing.net/gradient-
    generator/
2.  import turtle
3.
4.  myPen = turtle.Turtle()
5.  myPen.speed(0)
6.
7.  # This function draws a square of a given size and color
8.  def box(size,r,g,b):
9.      myPen.color(r,g,b)
10.     myPen.begin_fill()
11.     myPen.forward(size)
12.     myPen.left(90)
13.     myPen.forward(size)
14.     myPen.left(90)
15.     myPen.forward(size)
16.     myPen.left(90)
17.     myPen.forward(size)
18.     myPen.end_fill()
19.     myPen.setheading(0)
20.
21. #Position myPen in top left area of the screen
```

```
22. myPen.penup()
23. myPen.goto(-200,0)
24. myPen.pendown()
25.
26. #Retrieve user inputs: RGB colour codes of first and last co
    lour in the gradient
27. colorStartRed = int(input("RGB Code for color 1: Red (0-
    255): "))
28. colorStartGreen = int(input("RGB Code for color 1: Green (0-
    255): "))
29. colorStartBlue = int(input("RGB Code for color 1: Blue (0-
    255): "))
30. colorEndRed = int(input("RGB Code for color 2: Red (0-
    255): "))
31. colorEndGreen = int(input("RGB Code for color 2: Green (0-
    255): "))
32. colorEndBlue = int(input("RGB Code for color 2: Blue (0-
    255): "))
33.
34. #Let's calculate the RGB colour codes for each colour in the
    gradient
35. for i in range(0,8):
36.     red = colorStartRed + i * (colorEndRed-colorStartRed)/7
37.     green = colorStartGreen + i * (colorEndGreen-
    colorStartGreen)/7
38.     blue = colorStartBlue + i * (colorEndBlue-
    colorStartBlue)/7
39.     box(50, red, green, blue)
40.     myPen.penup()
41.     myPen.forward(50)
42.     myPen.pendown()
```

96. Python Fractals

A fractal is a curve or geometrical figure, which is based on a recurring pattern that repeats itself indefinitely at progressively smaller scales. Fractals are useful in modelling some structures (such as snowflakes), and in describing partly random or chaotic phenomena such as crystal growth and galaxy formation.

In this challenge we will be looking at two well-known fractals both named after the Polish mathematician Wacław Sierpiński:

- Sierpiński Triangle
- Sierpiński Carpet

Our aim is to use Python Turtle to reproduce the patterns of these two fractals on screen.

Web Address

http://www.101computing.net/python-fractals/

Sierpiński Triangle

The following figures show how the pattern of this fractal:

Python Code

```
1.  #Sierpinski Triangle - www.101computing.net/python-
    fractals/
2.  import turtle
3.
4.  myPen = turtle.Turtle()
5.  myPen.ht()
6.  myPen.speed(5)
7.  myPen.pencolor('black')
8.
9.  points = [[-175,-125],[0,175],[175,-
    125]] #Starting triangle
10.
11. def getMid(p1,p2):
12.   return ( (p1[0]+p2[0]) / 2, (p1[1] + p2[1]) / 2) #Find mid
    point coordinates
13.
14. def triangle(points,depth):
15.   myPen.up()
16.   myPen.goto(points[0][0],points[0][1])
17.   myPen.down()
18.   myPen.goto(points[1][0],points[1][1])
```

```
19.    myPen.goto(points[2][0],points[2][1])
20.    myPen.goto(points[0][0],points[0][1])
21.
22.    if depth>0:
23.        triangle([points[0],
24.        getMid(points[0], points[1]),
25.        getMid(points[0], points[2])],depth-1)
26.        triangle([points[1],getMid(points[0], points[1]),getMid(
    points[1], points[2])],depth-1)
27.        triangle([points[2],getMid(points[2], points[1]),getMid(
    points[0], points[2])],depth-1)
28.        `
29. triangle(points,4)
```

Sierpiński Carpet

The following figures show how the pattern of this fractal:

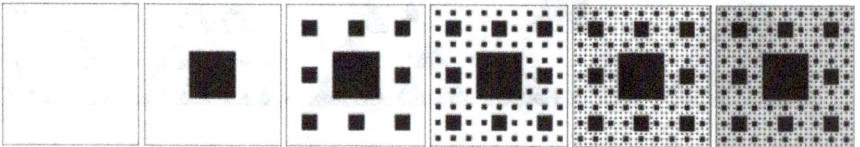

Python Code

```
1.  #Sierpinski Triangle - www.101computing.net/python-
    fractals/
2.  import turtle
3.
4.  myPen = turtle.Turtle()
5.  myPen.speed(10)
6.  myPen.color("#000000")
7.
8.  def square(boxSize,depth,x,y):
9.      myPen.penup()
10.     myPen.goto(x,y)
11.     myPen.pendown()
12.     myPen.begin_fill()
13.     myPen.forward(boxSize)
14.     myPen.left(90)
15.     myPen.forward(boxSize)
16.     myPen.left(90)
17.     myPen.forward(boxSize)
18.     myPen.left(90)
19.     myPen.forward(boxSize)
```

213

```
20.     myPen.end_fill()
21.     myPen.setheading(0)
22.     x1=x
23.     y1=y
24.
25.     if depth>0:
26.       size=boxSize/3
27.       x = x1 + (size)
28.       y = y1 - (2*(size))
29.       square(size,depth-1,x,y)
30.       x = x1 + boxSize + boxSize/3
31.       y = y1 - ((boxSize/3)*2)
32.       square(size,depth-1,x,y)
33.       x = x1 + boxSize + (boxSize/3)
34.       y = y1 + (boxSize/3)
35.       square(size,depth-1,x,y)
36.       x = x1 + boxSize + (boxSize/3)
37.       y = y1 + boxSize + (boxSize/3)
38.       square(size,depth-1,x,y)
39.       x = x1 + (boxSize/3)
40.       y = y1 + boxSize + (boxSize/3)
41.       square(size,depth-1,x,y)
42.       x = x1 - ((boxSize/3)*2)
43.       y = y1 + boxSize + (boxSize/3)
44.       square(size,depth-1,x,y)
45.       x = x1 - ((boxSize/3)*2)
46.       y = y1 + (boxSize/3)
47.       square(size,depth-1,x,y)
48.       x = x1 - ((boxSize/3)*2)
49.       y = y1 - ((boxSize/3)*2)
50.       square(size,depth-1,x,y)
51.
52. square(100,4,-50,-50)
```

97. Beach Huts Challenge

For this challenge we will use Python Turtle to draw three rows of beach huts.

The first row will use a sequence of four colours and repeat the sequence.

The second row will randomly pick one of the four colours for each hut.

The third row will be similar to the second row, using random colours but our program will make sure that two neighbouring huts cannot have the same colour.

Here is an example of the expected output of our program:

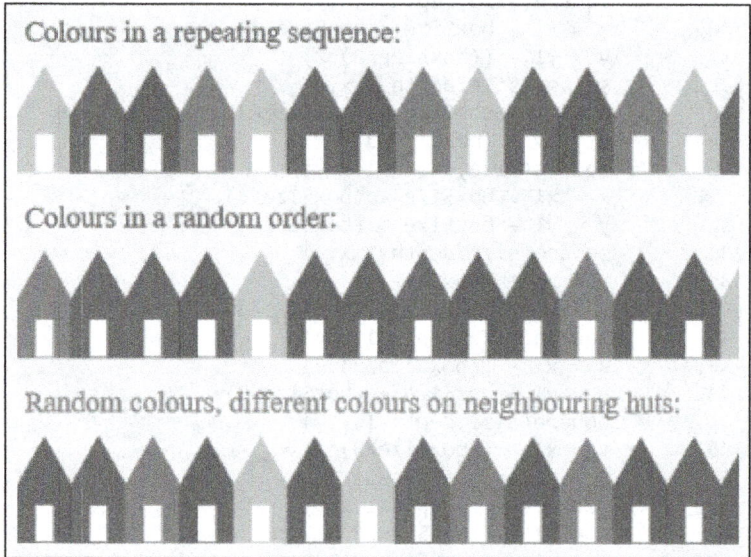

Colours in a repeating sequence:

Colours in a random order:

Random colours, different colours on neighbouring huts:

Web Address
http://www.101computing.net/beach-huts-challenge/

Python Code

```
1.  # Beach Huts Challenge - www.101computing.net/beach-huts-
    challenge/
2.  from turtle import *
3.  from random import randint
4.
5.  myPen = Turtle()
6.  myPen.shape("turtle")
7.  myPen.speed(0)
8.  myPen.tracer(0)
9.  myPen.hideturtle()
10.
```

```python
11. #A procedure to draw a beach hut of a given colour and at a
    given position
12. def beachHut(x,y,color):
13.   myPen.penup()
14.   myPen.goto(x,y)
15.   myPen.color(color)
16.   myPen.fillcolor(color)
17.   myPen.pendown()
18.   myPen.begin_fill()
19.   myPen.setheading(0)
20.   myPen.forward(30)
21.   myPen.left(90)
22.   myPen.forward(30)
23.   myPen.left(30)
24.   myPen.forward(30)
25.   myPen.left(120)
26.   myPen.forward(30)
27.   myPen.left(30)
28.   myPen.forward(30)
29.   myPen.end_fill()
30.   myPen.left(90)
31.   myPen.forward(10)
32.   myPen.fillcolor("#FFFFFF")
33.   myPen.pendown()
34.   myPen.begin_fill()
35.   myPen.penup()
36.   myPen.forward(10)
37.   myPen.left(90)
38.   myPen.forward(20)
39.   myPen.left(90)
40.   myPen.forward(10)
41.   myPen.left(90)
42.   myPen.forward(20)
43.   myPen.end_fill()
44.   myPen.penup()
45.
46. colorList = ["#82E0FF","#FF002B","#7C69FA","#F7639E"]
47. myPen.penup()
48.
49. #First row of beach huts
50. myPen.color("#FF002B")
51. myPen.goto(-196, 170)
52. myPen.write("Colours in a repeating sequence:", None, None,
    "12pt bold")
53.
54. colorIndex = 0
55. xPos = -200
56. yPos = 100
57.
```

```
58. for i in range(1,16):
59.   beachHut(xPos,yPos,colorList[colorIndex])
60.   colorIndex += 1
61.   if colorIndex == len(colorList):
62.     colorIndex = 0
63.   xPos += 30
64.
65. #Second row of beach huts - using random colours
66. myPen.color("#7C69FA")
67. myPen.goto(-196, 70)
68. myPen.write("Colours in a random order:", None, None, "12pt
    bold")
69.
70. colorIndex = len(colorList)-1
71. xPos = -200
72. yPos = 0
73.
74. for i in range(1,16):
75.   beachHut(xPos,yPos,colorList[colorIndex])
76.   colorIndex = randint(0, len(colorList)-1)
77.   xPos += 30
78.
79. #Third row of beach huts using random colours - no
80. myPen.color("#F7639E")
81. myPen.goto(-196, -30)
82. myPen.write("Random colours, different colours on neighbouri
    ng huts:", None, None, "12pt bold")
83.
84. previousColorIndex = -1
85. xPos = -200
86. yPos = -100
87.
88. for i in range(1,16):
89.   colorIndex = randint(0, len(colorList)-1)
90.   #Check if the same colour was used for the previous hut pr
      eviously
91.   while colorIndex==previousColorIndex:
92.     #Pick another colour
93.     colorIndex = randint(0, len(colorList)-1)
94.
95.   beachHut(xPos,yPos,colorList[colorIndex])
96.   #Tweak this code so that you cannot have two beach huts of
      the same colour next to each other.
97.
98.   previousColorIndex = colorIndex
99.   xPos += 30
100.
101.myPen.getscreen().update()
```

98. 3D Molecules

In this challenge we will use Glowscript to create a 3D animation representing the molecule CH₄ (Methane).

You can test a similar script, used to represent and animate the molecule H_2O (water) at the web address given below.

In the code given below we are creating the molecule CH₄ by joining five spheres together (one sphere for each atom, one cylinder for each link between two atoms). We then create a compound object to join these five spheres and four cylinders together in a single object (our molecule). Finally, using an infinite while loop, we animate/rotate the molecule around itself.

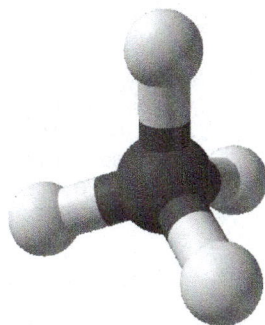

Web Address

http://www.101computing.net/3d-molecules/

Python Code

```
1.  #CH4 Molecule: 3D animation using Glowscript -
    www.101computing.net/3D-Molecules
2.
3.  #Build the molecule
4.  carbon=sphere(color=vector(1,1,0),pos=vec(0,0,0),radius=1.2,
    shininess=10)
5.  hydrogen1=sphere(color=vector(0,1,1),pos=vec(3,-1.5,-
    1),radius=1, shininess=10)
6.  hydrogen2=sphere(color=vector(0,1,1),pos=vec(-1,3,-
    1),radius=1, shininess=10)
7.  hydrogen3=sphere(color=vector(0,1,1),pos=vec(-3,-1.5,0-
    1),radius=1, shininess=10)
8.  hydrogen4=sphere(color=vector(0,1,1),pos=vec(0,0,3),radius=1
    , shininess=10)
9.
10. link1 = cylinder(pos=vector(0,0,0), axis=vector(3,-1.5,-
    1), radius=0.2)
```

```
11. link2 = cylinder(pos=vector(0,0,0), axis=vector(-1,3,-
    1), radius=0.2)
12. link3 = cylinder(pos=vector(0,0,0), axis=vector(-3,-1.5,-
    1), radius=0.2)
13. link4 = cylinder(pos=vector(0,0,0), axis=vector(0,0,3), radi
    us=0.2)
14.
15. molecule = compound([carbon,hydrogen1,hydrogen2, hydrogen3,
    hydrogen4, link1, link2, link3, link4])
16.
17. theta=0.1
18. framerate=20
19.
20. #Start the Animation
21. while True:
22.   rate(framerate)
23.   molecule.rotate(angle=theta, axis=vector(1,1,1), origin=ve
    ctor(0,0,0))
```

99. 3D Animation - Solar System

For this challenge, we will use Glowscript to create a
3D animation representing the revolution of some of
the planets around the Sun, and of the Moon around
the Earth.

Earth Revolution:

First, let's calculate the angle of rotation needed to rotate the Earth
around the Sun between two frames:

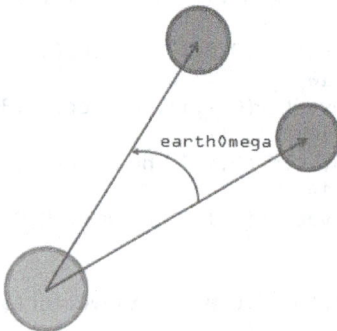

Duration (in days)	Revolution Angle (in radians)
365	$2 \times \Pi$
1	$\dfrac{2 \times \Pi}{365}$

$$earthOmega = \dfrac{2 \times \Pi}{365}$$

We will use this angle of rotation (earthOmega) in our 3D animation.

We will use a similar approach to calculate the angle of rotation of other planets based on their orbital periods: the orbital period of a planet corresponds to the number of days it takes for a planet to complete its revolution around the sun.

As not all planets orbit on the same 2D plan, we will modify the trajectory of our planets to take into consideration the orbital inclination of each planet.

Finally, we know that the revolution of a planet around the sun does not follow a circular orbit but an elliptic orbit. However for our model we will keep a circular trajectory for each planet orbiting around the Sun.

Here is the data that our model will use:

Planet	Orbital Period	Orbital Inclination
Mercury	88 Days	7.01°
Venus	225 Days	3.39°
Earth	35 Days	0°
Mars	687 Days	1.85°
Moon	28 Days	5.14°

Web Address

http://www.101computing.net/solar-system/

Python Code

```
1.  #Solar System 3D Animation using Glowscript -
    www.101computing.net/solar-system/
2.
3.  #Create 3D planets
4.  sun=sphere(color=vector(1,1,0),pos=vec(0,0,0),radius=1.5, sh
    ininess=10)
5.  mercury=sphere(color=vector(0,1,1),pos=vec(3,0,0),radius=0.4
    , shininess=10, make_trail=True)
```

```
 6.  venus=sphere(color=vector(1,0.6,0),pos=vec(7,0,0),radius=1,
     shininess=10, make_trail=True)
 7.  earth=sphere(color=vector(0,0,1),pos=vec(10,0,0),radius=1, s
     hininess=10, make_trail=True)
 8.  mars=sphere(color=vector(1,0.3,0),pos=vec(13,0,0),radius=0.5
     , shininess=10, make_trail=True)
 9.  moon=sphere(color=vector(0.5,0.5,0.5),pos=vec(12,0,0),radius
     =0.25, shininess=10, make_trail=True)
10.
11.  earth.make_trail=True
12.  moon.make_trail=False
13.  mercury.make_trail=True
14.  venus.make_trail=True
15.  mars.make_trail=True
16.
17.  #Calculating angles of rotation between two frames
18.  thetaEarth=2*3.14159/365
19.  thetaMercury=2*3.14159/88
20.  thetaVenus=2*3.14159/225
21.  thetaMars=2*3.14159/687
22.
23.  framerate=50
24.  omega=2*3.14159/28
25.  angle=0
26.
27.  #Calculating Orbital Inclination Vectors
28.  earthInclination = vector(0,1,0)
29.  mercuryInclination = vector(-
     sin(radians(7.01)),cos(radians(7.01)),0)
30.  venusInclination = vector(-
     sin(radians(3.99)),cos(radians(3.99)),0)
31.  marsInclination = vector(-
     sin(radians(1.85)),cos(radians(1.85)),0)
32.  moonInclination = vector(-
     sin(radians(5.14)),cos(radians(5.14)),0)
33.
34.  sunlight = local_light(pos=vector(0,0,0), color=color.yellow
     )
35.
36.  #Animate the planets
37.  days=0
38.  while True:
39.    days+=1
40.
41.    rate(framerate)
42.    #Planets orbit the Sun
43.    earth.rotate(angle=thetaEarth, axis=earthInclination, orig
     in=vector(0,0,0))
```

```
44.   mercury.rotate(angle=thetaMercury, axis=mercuryInclination
      , origin=vector(0,0,0))
45.   venus.rotate(angle=thetaVenus, axis=venusInclination, orig
      in=vector(0,0,0))
46.   mars.rotate(angle=thetaMars, axis=marsInclination, origin=
      vector(0,0,0))
47.
48.   #The Moon orbit the Earth
49.   angle+=omega
50.   moon.pos=earth.pos + vector(2,0,0)
51.   moon.rotate(angle=angle, axis=moonInclination, origin=eart
      h.pos)
```

100. 3D Rotating House

The aim of this challenge is to draw a house in 3D and

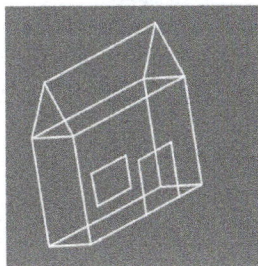

to make it rotate on the screen. Drawing 3D shapes on a screen (2D) requires some mathematical formulas to convert 3D (x,y,z) coordinates into 2D coordinates (x,y). This conversion also known as "oblique projection" is a great application of trigonometry, especially of the SOCATOA formulas:

$$\cos A = \frac{\text{adjacent}}{\text{hypotenuse}} = \frac{b}{c}.$$

$$\sin A = \frac{\text{opposite}}{\text{hypotenuse}} = \frac{a}{c}.$$

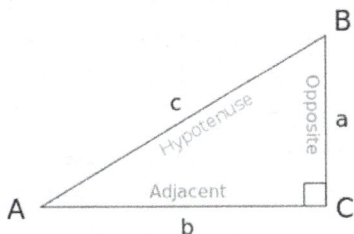

The oblique projection results in the following formulas:

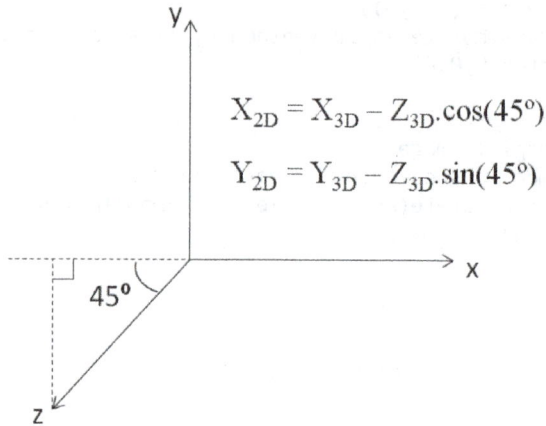

$$X_{2D} = X_{3D} - Z_{3D}.\cos(45°)$$

$$Y_{2D} = Y_{3D} - Z_{3D}.\sin(45°)$$

A 3D rotation against an axis (X, Y or Z axis) also requires some complex mathematical formulas.

To apply a 3D rotation we can use the rotation matrix as detailed on the right.

$$R_x(\theta) = \begin{bmatrix} 1 & 0 & 0 \\ 0 & \cos\theta & -\sin\theta \\ 0 & \sin\theta & \cos\theta \end{bmatrix}$$

In this challenge, to decide the angle and axis of rotation, we will use the position of the mouse pointer. The X coordinate of the mouse pointer becomes the angle of rotation against the Y axis. The Y coordinate of the mouse pointer becomes the angle of rotation against the X axis. In this example we will not implement a rotation against the Z axis.

$$R_y(\theta) = \begin{bmatrix} \cos\theta & 0 & \sin\theta \\ 0 & 1 & 0 \\ -\sin\theta & 0 & \cos\theta \end{bmatrix}$$

$$R_z(\theta) = \begin{bmatrix} \cos\theta & -\sin\theta & 0 \\ \sin\theta & \cos\theta & 0 \\ 0 & 0 & 1 \end{bmatrix}$$

You can find out more about the rotation matrix, on https://en.wikipedia.org/wiki/Rotation_matrix

Web Address

http://www.101computing.net/3d-challenge/

223

```
1.  # 3D Challenge - www.101computing.net/3D-challenge/
2.  #This house rotates based on the position of the mouse point
    er.
3.
4.  from processing import *
5.  from math import cos, sin, radians
6.
7.  X = 30
8.  Y = 30
9.  delay = 10
10. xCenter=200
11. yCenter=200
12.
13. def setup():
14.     strokeWeight(2)
15.     frameRate(20)
16.     size(400,400)
17.
18. #Each cube edge takes 6 coordinates: (xA,yA,zA,xB,yB,zB) to
    draw a line from A to B (2 corners of the cube)
19. #A cube is made of 12 edges:
20. cubeEdges=[[0,0,0,100,0,0]]
21. cubeEdges.append([100,0,0,100,100,0])
22. cubeEdges.append([100,100,0,0,100,0])
23. cubeEdges.append([0,100,0,0,0,0])
24. cubeEdges.append([0,0,100,100,0,100])
25. cubeEdges.append([100,0,100,100,100,100])
26. cubeEdges.append([100,100,100,0,100,100])
27. cubeEdges.append([0,100,100,0,0,100])
28. cubeEdges.append([0,0,0,0,0,100])
29. cubeEdges.append([0,100,0,0,100,100])
30. cubeEdges.append([100,100,0,100,100,100])
31. cubeEdges.append([100,0,0,100,0,100])
32. #Add Roof
33. cubeEdges.append([0,100,0,0,150,50])
34. cubeEdges.append([0,150,50,0,100,100])
35. cubeEdges.append([100,100,0,100,150,50])
36. cubeEdges.append([100,150,50,100,100,100])
37. cubeEdges.append([0,150,50,100,150,50])
38. #Add a Door
39. cubeEdges.append([20,0,0,20,50,0])
40. cubeEdges.append([20,50,0,50,50,0])
41. cubeEdges.append([50,50,0,50,0,0])
42. #Add a window
43. cubeEdges.append([60,30,0,60,60,0])
44. cubeEdges.append([60,60,0,90,60,0])
45. cubeEdges.append([90,60,0,90,30,0])
```

```
46. cubeEdges.append([90,30,0,60,30,0])
47.
48. def drawLine2D(edge):
49.    #This function converts the 3D coordinates (x,y,z) of both
       the starting position and end position of a line into 2D co
       ordinates (x,y)
50.    x2D_start = edge[0] + edge[2]*cos(radians(45)) + xCenter
51.    y2D_start = edge[1] - edge[2]*sin(radians(45)) + yCenter
52.    x2D_end = edge[3] + edge[5]*cos(radians(45)) + xCenter
53.    y2D_end = edge[4] -edge[5]*sin(radians(45)) + yCenter
54.    line(x2D_start,y2D_start,x2D_end,y2D_end)
55.
56. def startGame():
57.    global X, Y
58.    background(92,131,237)
59.    fill(255,255,255)
60.
61.    #Draw the goal line and the two posts
62.    stroke(255,255,255)
63.    X = (mouse.x);
64.    Y = (mouse.y);
65.    for cubeEdge in cubeEdges:
66.       edge=[cubeEdge[0],cubeEdge[1],cubeEdge[2],cubeEdge[3],
       cubeEdge[4],cubeEdge[5]]
67.       #Rotation Formula following X Axis.
68.       #The angle of rotation is based on the Y postion of th
       e mouse pointer.
69.       #These formulas are based on the Rotation Matrix
70.       y=edge[1]
71.       z=edge[2]
72.       edge[1]=y*cos(radians(Y)) - z*sin(radians(Y))
73.       edge[2]=y*sin(radians(Y)) + z*cos(radians(Y))
74.       y=edge[4]
75.       z=edge[5]
76.       edge[4]=y*cos(radians(Y)) - z*sin(radians(Y))
77.       edge[5]=y*sin(radians(Y)) + z*cos(radians(Y))
78.
79.       #Rotation Formula following Y Axis.
80.       #The angle of rotation is based on the X postion of th
       e mouse pointer.
81.       #These formulas are based on the Rotation Matrix

82.       z=edge[2]
83.       x=edge[0]
84.       edge[2]=z*cos(radians(X)) - x*sin(radians(X))
85.       edge[0]=z*sin(radians(X)) + x*cos(radians(X))
86.       z=edge[5]
87.       x=edge[3]
88.       edge[5]=z*cos(radians(X)) - x*sin(radians(X))
```

```
89.        edge[3]=z*sin(radians(X)) + x*cos(radians(X))
90.
91.        drawLine2D(edge)
92.
93.      fc = environment.frameCount
94.
95. draw = startGame
96. run()
```

Chapter #10: Object Oriented Programming

All previous 100 challenges are based on procedural programming. It is essential that you are fully confident with all the techniques we covered so far before moving on to the next stage of programming known as **OOP: Object Oriented Programming**.

The aim of this last challenge is not to teach all of the concepts of OOP programming. This challenge will however provide a basic introduction to what Object Oriented Programming is. It will also invite you to use the **PyGame library**, an OOP library specifically designed to add a Graphical User Interface (GUI) to your programs. This library will allow you to start creating your own video games.

This last challenge will focus on:

- Classes and Objects,
- Methods and Properties,
- PyGame Library,
- Creating our first game based on a Graphical User Interface (GUI).

101. Car Racing Game

Now that you have learned the basics of Python, you are most likely willing to start creating your own 2D or 3D video games. To do so, you will need to investigate available libraries such as the Pygame library (to create 2D games) or the OpenGL library to create 3D games.

Pygame is one of the best libraries to create mainly 2D retro arcade games such as Tetris, Breakout, PacMan or Space Invaders.
Before starting this project, you will need to download and install it following the instructions provided on the Pygame website:
http://www.pygame.org/

So far, all the challenges we have been working on are based on procedural programming. It is essential to be fully confident with procedural programming before attempting more complex projects. The next step is then to learn the key concepts of OOP (Object Oriented Programming).

For this challenge we are looking at creating a car racing game. The user will be able to control the car and move on the road between lanes by using the left and right arrow keys, accelerate or slow down using the up and down arrow keys. Other cars will be driving

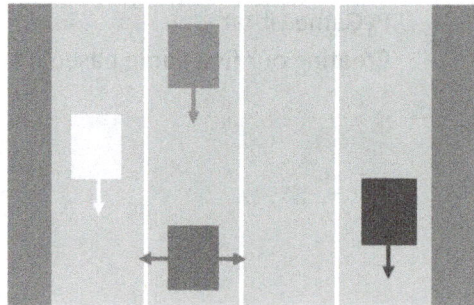

at a random speed from the top of the screen to the bottom of the screen. The aim of the car is to drive through these cars without causing a car crash.

In order to complete this project, we will with use the Pygame library and some Object Oriented Programming concepts. We will create our own Car class in a python file called *"car.py"*. We will import this class in our main program file called *"main.py"*. We will also create a *"popup.py"* library to store some of our generic functions.

Web Address

http://www.101computing.net/getting-started-with-pygame/

Download the Pygame Library

http://www.pygame.org/

Find out more about Object-Oriented Programming concepts

https://en.wikipedia.org/wiki/Object-oriented_programming

Python Code: Main Program: main.py

```
1.  import pygame, random
2.  #Let's import the Car Class
3.  from car import Car
4.  from popup import *
5.
6.  pygame.init()
7.
8.  GREEN = (20, 255, 140)
9.  GREY = (210, 210 ,210)
10. WHITE = (255, 255, 255)
11. RED = (255, 0, 0)
12. PURPLE = (255, 0, 255)
13. YELLOW = (255, 255, 0)
14. CYAN = (0, 255, 255)
15. BLUE = (100, 100, 255)
16. colorList = (RED, GREEN, PURPLE, YELLOW, CYAN, BLUE)
17.
18. #Initialise main variables
19. speed = 1
20. score=0
21. SCREENWIDTH=800
22. SCREENHEIGHT=600
23.
24. size = (SCREENWIDTH, SCREENHEIGHT)
25. screen = pygame.display.set_mode(size)
26. pygame.display.set_caption("Car Racing")
27.
28. #This will be a list that will contain all the sprites we in
    tend to use in our game.
```

```python
29. all_sprites_list = pygame.sprite.Group()
30.
31.
32. playerCar = Car(RED, 60, 80, 70)
33. playerCar.rect.x = 160
34. playerCar.rect.y = SCREENHEIGHT - 100
35.
36. car1 = Car(PURPLE, 60, 80, random.randint(50,100))
37. car1.rect.x = 60
38. car1.rect.y = -100
39.
40. car2 = Car(YELLOW, 60, 80, random.randint(50,100))
41. car2.rect.x = 160
42. car2.rect.y = -600
43.
44. car3 = Car(CYAN, 60, 80, random.randint(50,100))
45. car3.rect.x = 260
46. car3.rect.y = -300
47.
48. car4 = Car(BLUE, 60, 80, random.randint(50,100))
49. car4.rect.x = 360
50. car4.rect.y = -900
51.
52. # Add the car to the list of objects
53. all_sprites_list.add(playerCar)
54. all_sprites_list.add(car1)
55. all_sprites_list.add(car2)
56. all_sprites_list.add(car3)
57. all_sprites_list.add(car4)
58.
59. all_coming_cars = pygame.sprite.Group()
60. all_coming_cars.add(car1)
61. all_coming_cars.add(car2)
62. all_coming_cars.add(car3)
63. all_coming_cars.add(car4)
64.
65. #Allowing the user to close the window...
66. carryOn = True
67. clock=pygame.time.Clock()
68.
69. while carryOn:
70.         for event in pygame.event.get():
71.             if event.type==pygame.QUIT:
72.                 carryOn=False
73.             elif event.type==pygame.KEYDOWN:
74.                 if event.key==pygame.K_x:
75.                     playerCar.moveRight(10)
76.
77.         keys = pygame.key.get_pressed()
```

231

```
78.        if keys[pygame.K_LEFT]:
79.            playerCar.moveLeft(5)
80.        if keys[pygame.K_RIGHT]:
81.            playerCar.moveRight(5)
82.        if keys[pygame.K_UP]:
83.            speed += 0.05
84.        if keys[pygame.K_DOWN]:
85.            speed -= 0.05
86.
87.
88.        #Game Logic
89.        for car in all_coming_cars:
90.            car.moveForward(speed)
91.            if car.rect.y > SCREENHEIGHT:
92.                car.changeSpeed(random.randint(50,100))
93.                car.repaint(random.choice(colorList))
94.                car.rect.y = -200
95.                #Score 100 points per car
96.                score += 100
97.
98.        all_sprites_list.update()
99.
100.        #Check if there is a car collision
101.        car_collision_list = pygame.sprite.spritecollide(pla
    yerCar,all_coming_cars,False)
102.        for car in car_collision_list:
103.            print("Car crash!")
104.            popup(screen,"Game Over! Your Score: " + str(sco
    re) + " - Press enter key to quit.",360,40,350,200)
105.
106.            #End Of Game
107.            carryOn=False
108.
109.        #Drawing on Screen
110.        screen.fill(GREEN)
111.        #Draw The Road
112.        pygame.draw.rect(screen, GREY, [40,0, 400,SCREENHEIG
    HT])
113.        #Draw Line painting on the road
114.        pygame.draw.line(screen, WHITE, [140,0],[140,SCREENH
    EIGHT],5)
115.        pygame.draw.line(screen, WHITE, [240,0],[240,SCREENH
    EIGHT],5)
116.        pygame.draw.line(screen, WHITE, [340,0],[340,SCREENH
    EIGHT],5)
117.
118.        #Now let's draw all the sprites in one go. (For now
    we only have 1 sprite!)
119.        all_sprites_list.draw(screen)
```

```
120.
121.        #Refresh Screen
122.        pygame.display.flip()
123.
124.        #Number of frames per secong e.g. 60
125.        clock.tick(60)
126.
127.pygame.quit()
```

Python Code: Car Class: car.py

```
1.  import pygame
2.  WHITE = (255, 255, 255)
3.
4.  class Car(pygame.sprite.Sprite):
5.      #This class represents a car. It derives from the "Sprit
    e" class in Pygame.
6.
7.      def __init__(self, color, width, height, speed):
8.          # Call the parent class (Sprite) constructor
9.          super().__init__()
10.
11.         # Pass in the color of the car, and its x and y posi
    tion, width and height.
12.         # Set the background color and set it to be transpar
    ent
13.         self.image = pygame.Surface([width, height])
14.         self.image.fill(WHITE)
15.         self.image.set_colorkey(WHITE)
16.
17.         #Initialise attributes of the car.
18.         self.width=width
19.         self.height=height
20.         self.color = color
21.         self.speed = speed
22.
23.         # Draw the car (a rectangle!)
24.         pygame.draw.rect(self.image, self.color, [0, 0, self
    .width, self.height])
25.
26.         # Instead we could load a proper pciture of a car...

27.         # pygame.image.load("car.png").convert()
28.
29.         # Fetch the rectangle object that has the dimensions
     of the image.
30.         self.rect = self.image.get_rect()
```

233

```
31.
32.    def moveRight(self, pixels):
33.        self.rect.x += pixels
34.
35.    def moveLeft(self, pixels):
36.        self.rect.x -= pixels
37.
38.    def moveForward(self, speed):
39.        self.rect.y += self.speed * speed / 20
40.
41.    def moveBackward(self, speed):
42.        self.rect.y -= self.speed * speed / 20
43.
44.    def changeSpeed(self, speed):
45.        self.speed= speed
46.
47.    def repaint(self, color):
48.        self.color = color
49.        pygame.draw.rect(self.image, self.color, [0, 0, self
    .width, self.height])
```

Python Code: Popup Library: popup.py

```
1.  import pygame
2.  from pygame.locals import *
3.
4.  def getKey():
5.    #Wait for a key to be pressed
6.    while 1:
7.      event = pygame.event.poll()
8.      if event.type == pygame.KEYDOWN:
9.        return event.key
10.     else:
11.       pass
12.
13. def popup(screen, message, width=300, height=40, x=200, y=20
    0, bgColor=(255,0,0), textColor=(255,255,255)):
14.   #Display a popup box in the middle of the screen
15.
16.   fontobject = pygame.font.Font(None,18)
17.   pygame.draw.rect(screen, bgColor,
18.                    (x - width/2 +2,
19.                     y - height/2 +2,
20.                     width,height-4), 0)
21.   pygame.draw.rect(screen, (255,255,255),
22.                    (x - width/2,
23.                     y - height/2,
```

```
24.                    width+4,height), 1)
25.    if len(message) != 0:
26.      screen.blit(fontobject.render(message, 1, textColor),
27.                (x - width/2 + 10, y - height/2 + 14))
28.    pygame.display.flip()
29.    #This popup will only disappear when the user presses the
    Return key
30.    while 1:
31.      inkey = getKey()
32.      if inkey == pygame.K_RETURN:
33.        break
```

Made in the USA
Monee, IL
08 January 2025

76388558R00134